THE SUNDAY TIMES

Book of
Jubilee Year

THE SUNDAY TIMES

Book of Jubilee Year

EDITED BY
HUNTER DAVIES

MICHAEL JOSEPH
LONDON

First published in Great Britain by
Michael Joseph Limited
52 Bedford Square
London WC1B 3EF
1977

ISBN 0 7181 1672 0

Filmset by Filmtype Services Ltd, Scarborough
Printed in Great Britain by
Beric Press Ltd, Crawley, Sussex
and bound by Dorstel Press Ltd, Harlow

Contents

Introduction

The Silver Jubilee produced the most spontaneous out-pouring of national enjoyment since the end of the Second World War. During 1977 the people of Great Britain and the Commonwealth put aside their problems for a brief while and joined together to celebrate the twenty-fifth anniversary of the Queen's reign. Even the most hardened anti-royalist cynic was confounded by the upsurge of genuine affection. Even those most doom-laden by the economic crisis of the time had to admit, despite a certain apathy in the early part of the year, that during June the whole country was involved and excited by the pomp and the pageantry. The Jubilee, for a moment, provided a tonic and uplift for the nation.

For the first time, the leading participants in a Jubilee celebration went walkabout, an unattractive term, but a very attractive notion, one so obvious, so pleasing to the viewers, that afterwards it seemed strange that our Royal family had hardly indulged in it before. The nation caught the spirit of delight and informality, and the streets and shops throughout the country went Jubilee mad. Most of all, it was fun. The street parties, if nothing else, will live for ever in the memory of all those who took part. For once it was not a war which had brought neighbours out and into the streets and into each others celebrations.

This is the record of the year's major events, seen through the eyes of some of the world's leading photographers. *The Sunday Times Magazine* brought seventeen eminent photographers to London for the Jubilee celebrations. They included Henri Cartier-Bresson, Martine Franck, Marc Riboud from France; Eve Arnold and Robert Freson from the USA; Georg Gerster from Switzerland; Kenneth Griffiths from New Zealand; Donald McCullin, Ian Berry,

Roger Perry, David Reed, Ian Yeomans and Alain le Garsmeur from Britain. Together, they took 15,000 photographs. The work of many other photographers, such as Anwar Hussein, and of Press agencies has also been called upon, from Britain and the Commonwealth.

Hunter Davies, editor of *The Sunday Times Magazine*, has selected the photographs and written a commentary which charts and describes the progress of the year. It starts in February with the Queen's tour of the Pacific, New Zealand and Australia, returns to Britain for the tour of Scotland, and then in June moves into the events of Jubilee Week itself – the Royal procession, the service at St Paul's Cathedral, the fireworks and river pageantry. The street parties, up and down the country, are recaptured, as are the decorations and displays. There are also special chapters on the Queen's tour of Wales and the rest of England, on the Naval Review at Spithead and on Prince Charles's tour of Canada, plus a section on the sporting events at which the Queen was present, such as the Derby and the Wimbledon Ladies' Singles Final which Virginia Wade won.

It was a very colourful year. The richness and breadth of the Queen's world-wide Jubilee celebrations can only be captured in colour photographs, souvenirs in themselves, which can be studied and enjoyed for ever. It was the sort of occasion we will look back at in the years ahead and wonder at the faces and the clothes, the buildings and the people, long after they have gone, long after the world has moved on. Perhaps, who knows, such pomp and pageantry might never be seen on such a scale again. With the Queen as our guide, this is a slice of social history, a record of an exceptional year.

Ceremonial splendour: the Queen and Prince Philip in the uniform of the Noble Order of the Thistle, Edinburgh, May 1977

Duty calls: Coronation Day, 1953. For the first time in half a century the Sovereign was a woman

The Royal House of Windsor

It's possible to trace the royal line back to Cerdic, King of the West Saxons in the sixth century, but it becomes tenuous at times. This Queen's family tree therefore starts with Queen Victoria. Her nine children linked so many European royal families that not all her descendants can be shown here. Prince Philip can also trace his roots to Victoria, the last Hanoverian monarch. The dynasty of the House of Windsor began with the Queen's grandfather, King George V

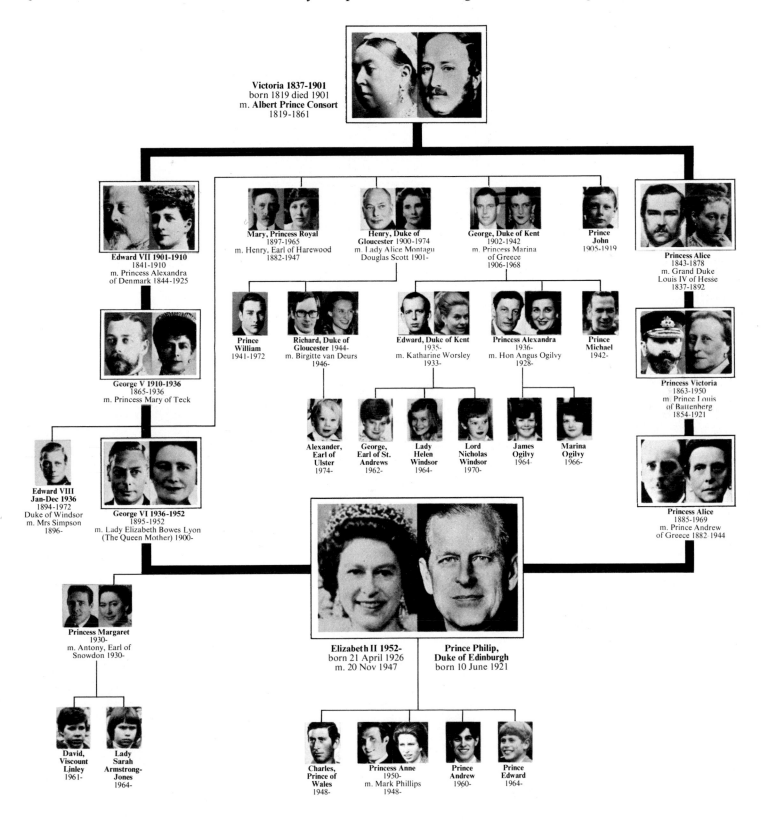

Victoria 1837-1901
born 1819 died 1901
m. **Albert Prince Consort**
1819-1861

Edward VII 1901-1910
1841-1910
m. Princess Alexandra
of Denmark 1844-1925

Mary, Princess Royal
1897-1965
m. Henry, Earl of Harewood
1882-1947

**Henry, Duke of
Gloucester 1900-1974**
m. Lady Alice Montagu
Douglas Scott 1901-

George, Duke of Kent
1902-1942
m. Princess Marina
of Greece
1906-1968

**Prince
John**
1905-1919

Princess Alice
1843-1878
m. Grand Duke
Louis IV of Hesse
1837-1892

George V 1910-1936
1865-1936
m. Princess Mary of Teck

**Prince
William**
1941-1972

**Richard, Duke of
Gloucester 1944-**
m. Birgitte van Deurs
1946-

Edward, Duke of Kent
1935-
m. Katharine Worsley
1933-

Princess Alexandra
1936-
m. Hon Angus Ogilvy
1928-

**Prince
Michael**
1942-

Princess Victoria
1863-1950
m. Prince Louis
of Battenberg
1854-1921

**Edward VIII
Jan-Dec 1936**
1894-1972
Duke of Windsor
m. Mrs Simpson
1896-

George VI 1936-1952
1895-1952
m. Lady Elizabeth Bowes Lyon
(The Queen Mother) 1900-

**Alexander,
Earl of
Ulster**
1974-

**George,
Earl of St.
Andrews**
1962-

**Lady
Helen
Windsor**
1964-

**Lord
Nicholas
Windsor**
1970-

**James
Ogilvy**
1964-

**Marina
Ogilvy**
1966-

Princess Alice
1885-1969
m. Prince Andrew
of Greece 1882-1944

Princess Margaret
1930-
m. Antony, Earl of
Snowdon 1930-

Elizabeth II 1952-
born 21 April 1926
m. 20 Nov 1947

**Prince Philip,
Duke of Edinburgh**
born 10 June 1921

**David,
Viscount
Linley**
1961-

**Lady
Sarah
Armstrong-
Jones**
1964-

**Charles,
Prince of
Wales**
1948-

Princess Anne
1950-
m. Mark Phillips
1948-

**Prince
Andrew**
1960-

**Prince
Edward**
1964-

CHAPTER ONE

The Year Begins

The year dawned grey and grim. There was economic gloom all around. General Amin appeared to be going mad in Uganda. Northern Ireland was still a nightmare. Amin had been partly a joke figure for many people in the previous year but now, in the New Year, there were reports coming through from Uganda of widespread murder. The IRA exploded seven fire-bombs at the end of January in London's Oxford Street, but nobody was killed. There seemed little prospect of a fun-filled year.

Even the Royal Family, in those cold January days, promised little cheer. A particularly boring photograph was wheeled out for the waiting scribes to plop in their newspapers and magazines. It is the tradition on great Royal events, such as birthdays and births, marriages and jubilees, that an "official" photograph is released. One newspaper or agency is allowed one sitting, on a rota basis, and then the results, duly vetted, are handed out for everyone to use, or in several cases this time, not use. So in January, an official photograph appeared to start Jubilee year. You see it on the left. It earns its place in these very competitive pages purely as a matter of record. It's a traditional, rather glazed pose but perhaps, after all, it was in keeping with the mood of January 1977.

The economic situation was indeed dire. There were more than 1·3 million unemployed; inflation was running at 16 per cent; and the January trade deficit was £545 million, the worst monthly trade-gap ever recorded. The Government tried muttering that the long Christmas holiday (when many people had contrived to have ten days off, not returning to work until January 4) was one of the main reasons, but nobody was convinced. The Prime Minister, Mr James Callaghan, and the Chancellor of the Exchequer, Mr Denis Healey, appeared jubilant when they announced on January 12 that they'd secured a loan of 3000 million dollars from the International Monetary Fund, and they promised firm control of prices, wages and government spending. All the same, Jubilee year looked like being expensive. Plastic carrier bags, normally 3p, jumped to 15p, thanks to the addition of a Union Jack.

Prince Philip, usually so ready with a cheerful retort, wasn't much help. "The economic situation in Britain is rather like dry rot in a building," he was reported as saying in the *Director* magazine of January 18. "You don't know when it starts, you don't know when the crisis is, but gradually the place becomes uninhabitable." He maintained he was still confident about the prospects for recovery, but it was a fairly strong speech, at least for the Queen's consort to make.

However, there were two definite rays of hope as the year began. North Sea oil was seen at last to be flowing black and strong. The January figures showed that Britain was now producing more than 25 per cent of her own oil – and it was even predicted that £400m worth of crude oil would be exported in 1977. They were particularly pleased in Scotland, where the newly dynamic Scottish National Party had already laid claim to it all being Scottish oil.

Tourism was also reported to be entering its best year ever. The British Tourist Authority announced that £2100 million had been earned from tourism in 1976 and that it would shoot up to £2700 in 1977 – the equivalent of £7m a day from tourists. The Jubilee was expected to bring in more than 11,400,000 overseas visitors during the year. Despite those grey, grim January days, the plastic carrier bag-makers and bunting manufacturers were working as loyally and feverishly as possible.

★　★　★　★　★

The Queen saw her Jubilee year in with her family at Sandringham, where she spent most of January. There were no public engagements and she quietly prepared herself for the year ahead. It would be her only relatively calm period of the year, but she had lots of briefing and plans to master for the forthcoming massive Commonwealth tour.

General Amin stole lots of headlines by saying he was coming with a party of 250 to celebrate the Queen's Silver Jubilee and to see the Queen, "His Commander in Chief". There was a certain embarrassment from the Foreign Office and Buckingham Palace officials, who were forced to admit that in fact no official invitation was necessary – Amin could come if he wanted to, as a head of state, to the Commonwealth Conference.

The Sex Pistols, a group of young people playing a form of pop music called punk rock, made themselves notorious by swearing on TV and spitting out rude remarks about the Queen and the Jubilee. Naturally enough, the Queen did not pass any remarks. But, surprisingly, she expressed her public disapproval about the proposed plans of a Danish film maker, Jens Jorgen Thorsen, to make a film about the sex life of Jesus. It wasn't that her views were surprising in

Royal tradition: the 'official' Press photograph of the Queen in the library at Balmoral, released to start Jubilee year, January 1977

themselves – the country as a whole agreed with her – but that she allowed her views on the passing show to be made public, thereby ensuring more publicity.

In early February the newspapers started to announce final preparations for the Jubilee celebrations and there was immediately some criticism about the expense of it all. Tom Litterick, Labour MP for Selly Oak, Birmingham, denounced the Royal Family as "useless layabouts", after increases in the Queen's allowance were announced in an effort to keep them inflation-proof.

The Press looked back over the past twenty-five years, and in general it made depressing reading. In the twenty-five years, the pound had sunk to a true value of only 24p. Food was five times as expensive, and houses six times as expensive. Even so, one person in three now had a TV set, compared with one in sixty-six in 1951. Most of the population could therefore look forward to sitting at home and thrilling to the Jubilee on television.

Local councils were being very cagey about promising to spend any extra money in Jubilee year. Even the Royal Borough of Windsor was very cautious: "Previous jubilees have produced some very spectacular displays in the streets, but items such as triumphal arches are unlikely to be a viable proposition in the present economic climate." Many councils refused to spend anything on Jubilee celebrations.

The Times, under the headline "Jubilee trumpets are muted by financial misgivings", wondered if the unease about spending was caused by the fact that the Queen wasn't planning any symbolic Jubilee actions. After all, Edward III had granted pardons for prisoners; George III had given money to imprisoned debtors; Queen Victoria had released some political agitators; children had received free mugs when it was George V's jubilee in 1935. What was anyone going to get out of Elizabeth II's Jubilee? The answer, said Buckingham Palace, was an extra Bank Holiday in the summer.

The nation did get the benefit, for free, of the Poet Laureate's skills – and it didn't cost the Queen very much; all the Laureate gets is £70 a year. Sir John Betjeman produced his Jubilee hymn in early February, just before the Queen's departure. A rather unmagnanimous Tory MP, Nicholas Fairbairn, member for Kinross and Perthshire West, called it "banal" and said he could write a much better Jubilee hymn. Another Tory MP, Dr Rhodes Boyson, of Brent North, said it certainly seemed like poetry to him, "compared with much of the modern nonsense". The chorus of the hymn, to which the Master of the Queen's Musick, Malcolm Williamson, composed the music, went as follows:

> For our Monarch and her people
> United yet and free
> Let the bells from every steeple
> Ring out loud the Jubilee.

Sir John could at least take some consolation from the fact that his predecessor, Cecil Day-Lewis, also attracted much criticism for his Royal poetry.

★　★　★　★　★

On February 6, the Queen attended morning service at the Royal Chapel, Windsor, to mark the start of Silver Jubilee celebrations. It was the twenty-fifth anniversary, to the day, of her accession to the throne. The Queen was accompanied by Prince Philip, Prince Charles, Princess Anne, Prince Edward, the Queen Mother and Princess Margaret, and they were screened from view behind the Royal pew. For the Royal family, the service was a private family remembrance in memory of the death of George VI.

It was on February 6, 1952 that George VI had died. He had waved his daughter farewell only six days earlier as she'd departed on her Commonwealth tour. She was staying at Treetops, a small observation lodge high up in a fig tree in a Kenyan game-park, when the news came through. Commander Parker, Prince Philip's secretary, had learned it first from a local newspaper. He awoke Prince Philip, who was taking a siesta. "I never felt so sorry for anyone in my life," Parker later recalled. "He looked as if you'd dropped the world on him." Prince Philip kept the news to himself for an hour, fiddling with the radio to get confirmation. When it was at last confirmed, he told the Princess. At the age of twenty-five, against most expectations, she had become Queen. Her private life as a young married woman with two children was over. For the first time in half a century, since Queen Victoria's death in 1901, the Sovereign was a woman.

Now twenty-five years later, after twenty-five years as Queen, she was preparing for yet another Commonwealth tour. She wouldn't be going to Africa on this particular tour, but to Australia, New Zealand and the Pacific, a trip of some two months' duration. That evening, while the family were at dinner, President Carter sent a message from the United States, congratulating her on the occasion of the twenty-fifth anniversary of her succession.

★　★　★　★　★

The Queen and Prince Philip flew from London Airport at 10.25 pm on Wednesday, February 9, leaving the morning papers to wonder over the *Daily Mirror*'s latest revelations about the previous Prime Minister, Harold Wilson, and his Honours List. One of his ex-aides, Joe Haines, was alleging that it was the PM's secretary Marcia Williams, now Lady Falkender, who had drawn up the list – on purple notepaper. With such gossip around, the Queen's departure was hardly noticed.

In twenty-five years Commonwealth tours had become rather commonplace. It hadn't sunk in that this was the *Jubilee* tour, the real start of the Jubilee celebrations. On board the British Airways 707 aircraft was steward Kenneth 'Nobby' Clarke, who had looked after the Queen twenty-five years earlier when she had been brought back to England on the death of George VI.

The first Royal stop was in Western Samoa in the Pacific. Samoa was once the home of Robert Louis Stevenson and is still very much a treasure island, with beautiful beaches, bananas, breadfruits and coconuts. "You lie on a mat in a cool Samoan hut and look out on the white sand under the high palms. It is sheer beauty," wrote Rupert Brooke in 1913.

The islanders, some 170,000, were pleased to be the first port of call for the Jubilee Queen, though their leaders were becoming used to being pleased and feted. Both China and Russia were currently trying to increase their influence in Samoa and had been lavishly entertaining Samoan leaders. The Queen invited the Head of State, Malietoa Tanumafili, on board the Royal Yacht *Britannia*, which she had now joined, and knighted him. He had asked not to be knighted on Samoan soil and not to have to kneel down. Both wishes were granted. He in turn bestowed on the Queen the Grand Order of the Vailima, the name of Stevenson's home, meaning Meeting of Five Rivers.

On shore, the Queen received a great welcome. There were no security risks, though one local policeman, Constable Simanau, who wears the local dress of wrap-around skirts called *lavalavas*, had been quoted as saying that he was looking forward to the day when the Samoan police moved into trousers. "It's not easy in a skirt to fight a man with a dagger."

The crowds first greeted the Queen in silence, the traditional mark of great respect, then broke into songs. The local bands played a Samoan number which loses somewhat in translation: "You are the flower behind my ear and the necklace round my neck." The Head of State entertained the Royal couple to a huge banquet of sucking pig; the Samoans love overeating and take great pride in their girth. The Queen wore a simple cotton frock and chiffon headscarf; the Prince was even more informal in a gaudy, Polynesian green shirt. They obviously enjoyed the sun and informality and the gaiety, a pleasant relief from trade-gaps and unemployment figures and people being horrid about her Poet Laureate.

Next, on February 14, came a one-day stop on Tonga where there was more feasting and singing and Polynesian hospitality. A New Zealand frigate, *Taranaki*, which was accompanying *Britannia*, gave a 21-gun salute on arrival. The Tonga defence services replied with a shore battery gun, a present from Britain in 1947.

The King of Tonga turned out to be built on the same generous lines as his mother, Queen Salote, who had captivated the attention of many people during the Coronation celebrations. He has been known to weigh thirty-three stone and weighs himself on airport scales. For the occasion, though, he had lost fifty pounds. He entertained the Queen and Prince Philip to a feast of sucking pig, turkey, lobsters, water-melon and yams. Only he and his Queen, plus the British Royal couple, were given chairs. Everyone else had to sit cross-legged on the ground, which proved rather awkward for one of the Queen's ladies-in-waiting in a straight silk frock. She managed to retain her dignity by sitting sideways.

Tongan girls dressed in white fanned the Royal party throughout the meal, while footmen from *Britannia* sweltered in their lounge suits. The Queen, with great ceremony, was presented with her very own sucking pig to eat, as well as a turkey, two lobsters and her very own coconut. She was seen to shoot a deadpan glance at Prince Philip, and became so engrossed in all the activity and entertainment that she didn't have time to eat a lot, though she did manage a little chicken and pineapple.

They were so confident of good weather in Fiji, the third and final of the Polynesian stops, that they had made no bad-weather plans. The Waimaro tribe did their famed fine-weather ritual – and the result was torrential rain for the Queen's arrival. However, the weather didn't spoil the welcome and the ceremonies. The Queen was presented with six chairs and a table, and thanked her hosts most regally. "They are beautiful examples of Fijian craftsmanship. You may be quite sure that we shall use them." They were entertained by local chiefs who chanted "Oi" and "Aah" and clapped their hands. "As always," reported Ann Morrow in *The Daily Telegraph*, "the Queen manages to look as if she understands perfectly the language of the country she is in and also appears impressed by the profundity of the speaker."

All the men in the Royal party were noticed to be particularly impressed by a troupe of Bananas girls who did saucy dances in coconut bras with a lot of hip-twitching. During another ceremonial dance, a corrugated roof, covered with spectators, caved in. The Queen was seen to look alarmed by the noise of crashing, but no one was hurt.

★ ★ ★ ★ ★

The New Zealand tour started on February 22. The reality of life back home became apparent when on the eve of her arrival, New Zealand's Prime Minister, Robert Muldoon, announced his country's willingness to accept "refugees" from Northern Ireland, offering a home to Ulster people regardless of what they might have been involved in.

First stop in New Zealand was Auckland, the largest city, where the Queen began the first of her many Jubilee walkabouts. More than 10,000 people managed to see her at close quarters as she walked round Auckland before lunch. On seeing a badge pinned to Mrs Molly Frampton, in the crowd, she said: "You belong to the Women's Institute. So do I." Prince Philip managed some merrier quips to

The first of the Jubilee tours: the Queen and Prince Philip begin their Commonwealth tour. Their first stop was at Western Samoa, in the Pacific, February 1977

passers-by. "Are they kind to you?" he asked some Auckland Diocesan college schoolgirls. "Or do they whip you?" The girls collapsed in giggles.

At lunch, the Queen was given some twelve-year-old Sylvaner Riesling, saved specially for her and said to be her favourite drink. She received a warm welcome after lunch when visiting Ellerslie Racecourse, despite the presence of a banner saying "Anarchy not Monarchy". A noisy crowd of three, the owners of the banner, were placed by the police for safety behind some white gates.

Britannia then sailed to North Island, where again there were walkabouts, lunches, ceremonies, openings and speeches. It was noticed in New Zealand by observant Queen-watchers that the Queen no longer used the phrase "my husband", preferring instead either "Prince Philip" or "the Duke of Edinburgh". At Mystery Creek on North Island, an old Maori woman rushed up to the Queen and began telling her with wide swaying gestures some long, ancient legend. The Queen smiled broadly as the woman put her dark head on the Queen's shoulder, but the Queen's detective brought the chat carefully to a close, showing what was described as "consummate skill".

Later, at a ceremony in Gisborne, the Queen arrived at a Maori celebration wearing a cloak of Kiwi feathers, in complete contrast to her formal peach gaberdine dress and jacket and diamond and pearl clips. At the State Opening of Parliament in Wellington, the most formal occasion of the tour so far, the Queen was resplendent in full evening dress and ruby tiara – at 2.25 in the afternoon. The new Parliament buildings, designed by the late Sir Basil Spence, were not quite ready for the official opening. The Queen had trouble pulling a cord to unveil the plaque. She pulled again, but the curtains refused to move. She leaned forward, smiling and unperturbed, and opened the curtains by hand.

The Queen also managed to avoid any unpleasantness when she walked into a private room, set aside for her in Auckland, where a woman was going through her handbag. It turned out to be an overzealous policewoman.

At her farewell banquet in Christchurch, at the end of her two-week tour, the Queen spoke emotionally about "this beautiful and kindly country". She and Prince Philip had visited twenty New Zealand cities and towns, been on nineteen walkabouts and been seen by an estimated one million people, a third of the population. All the Royal officials and the New Zealand organisers were delighted at the success of the entire tour. "We have been very happy here and are sad to go," said the Queen.

★　★　★　★　★

Her Majesty couldn't have been all that happy on her arrival in Australia on March 7, though the handful of demonstrations she walked into were not aiming their abuse at her personally. Just over a year previously, the Queen's representative, Governor-General Sir John Kerr, had dismissed the Gough Whitlam government. There was still political disquiet over the dismissal and far from unanimous support for the new Prime Minister, Malcolm Fraser. The republican movement, which wanted Australia to cut all ties with the United Kingdom, had been gaining strength. On the eve of her arrival, a poll published in Australia said that 58 per cent felt they didn't need a Queen, 40 per cent were in favour and 2 per cent didn't know. Mr Fraser, reflecting the changing attitudes, decreed that Australians could now take their choice from three national anthems – *God Save the Queen, Waltzing Matilda* and *Advance Australia Fair*.

As the Queen took her first steps on Australian soil at Fairbairn air-base, a primary school teacher attempted to get his pupils to boo – but instead they cheered and clapped.

But there were boos at the opening of the second session of Parliament next day in Canberra. A small group of republicans, spotting Mr Fraser, booed him and the Queen as they walked up the steps. It could perhaps have had some effect on her. Despite 12-hour itineraries, endless travel, and endlessly having to be charming and interested and hungry, the Queen very rarely fluffs her lines. On this occasion she did. "It is with great pleasure I have returned to Australia in this Silver Jubilee reign of my year." Outside Parliament House, 300 demonstrators waved banners and shouted "Kerr is a Traitor." Gough Whitlam made a jocular reference to the Queen as the Queen of Sheba while the Queen managed a smile. He also referred to the United Kingdom as "now the lonely outpost of the Commonwealth".

In Brisbane a man with a foreign accent was reported to have threatened the Queen with a bomb attack, but nothing happened and 25,000 young people turned out in the rain to greet her. However, Mr Fraser's car was bombarded with empty beer-cans. In Sydney, the Queen was struck by a placard, the worst incident on the tour so far, but she played it down, chiding the Press for overstating what had happened. By the time she got to Melbourne, the crowds were universally jubilant and the Queen's decision to stick to her walkabout style was handsomely vindicated.

Australia had a three-day respite from cheering, or wondering about demonstrations, while the Queen and Prince Philip went to Papua-New Guinea, where the crowds were greater than anyone had expected. Papua, though newly independent and in search of identity, could wholeheartedly welcome the Queen, still their Head of State, without worrying too much about any political overtones.

The Royal couple then returned to Australia, finally leaving Perth Airport on March 30. "Kindness and friendship have been shown to us wherever we have been," said the Queen. "And if on occasions there has been a note of dissent, that is what freedom of expression is all about – a freedom sadly no longer enjoyed in many other countries."

The Queen in Samoa: the Royal couple were greeted by a deathly hush, the islanders' traditional mark of respect. But the crowds soon broke into songs, cheered themselves hoarse, and waved their Union Jacks

The friendly islands: Polynesi[an]
hospitality is extended to [the]
Queen by His Royal Highn[ess]
King Taufa'ahau Tupou IV, s[on]
of the late Queen Salote who st[ole]
the show at the Coronation

All the Queen's men: the pro[ud]
members of Tonga's defence s[er]
vices on parade for an inspecti[on]
by the Queen

The show goes on: the Queen and Prince Philip receive and are entertained by Fijian folk and traditional dancers on board the Royal Yacht *Britannia*

Cloak of friendship: in complete contrast to he[r]
Hardy Amies outfit, the Queen wears a cloak [of]
Kiwi feathers at a Maori ceremony at Gisborne[,]
New Zealand, 1977

top picture
Pet subject: the Queen spots a Corgi-owner in th[e]
crowd and has a chat about what is obviously the[r]
favourite topic. New Zealand, 1977

bottom picture
Knight of the realm: one of the more seriou[s]
ceremonies the Queen carried out was an investitu[re]
at Wellington, New Zealand, 1977

Decoration fit for a Knight: amid flowers, the Queen carried out an investiture ceremony at Wellington, and attended the formal State Opening of Parliament

Meeting the people: in New Zealand the Queen inspected the armed forces from an open Land Rover. When she moved on to Australia she met a parade of the Scouts' movement, and received the players of a football match

Happy and glorious: crowds in Sydney gave the Queen a rapturous welcome, but there was a nasty moment when Her Majesty was struck by an anti-royalist placard

CHAPTER TWO

Scotland

Small is beautiful was one of the clichés of the year. There was a move against big corporations, big comprehensives, big high-rise flats and big countries. People wanted to be part of small units. In Scotland and Wales it was called devolution, and for many months of 1977 it was fiercely debated in the House of Commons. The Scottish National Party had gone from strength to strength, becoming the biggest single party in Scotland with 36 per cent of the electorate on its side. The argument about whether Scotland should have a form of independence even led to a split in the Labour Party.

The Queen's tour of Scotland was planned to start on May 17 and it looked as if, unwittingly, she was going to walk into political trouble, just as she'd done in Australia. This time, most surprisingly, she entered the arena herself with a public, political statement. In a Silver Jubilee speech to Parliament on May 4, the Queen warned of the danger of a break-up of the United Kingdom, much to the annoyance of the Nationalist MPs.

> I number kings and queens of England and of Scotland and princes of Wales among my ancestors and so I can readily understand these aspirations. But I cannot forget that I was crowned Queen of the United Kingdom of Great Britain and Northern Ireland. Perhaps this Jubilee is a time to remind ourselves of the benefits which union has conferred, at home and in our international dealings, on the inhabitants of all parts of this United Kingdom.

As a speech from a politician, it would probably have been ignored. As Royal pronouncements go, it was fighting talk.

The Queen's Scottish tour began when she and Prince Philip arrived on the new Royal Train at Glasgow Central Station on May 17. Many people wondered if her reception would be cool if not hostile. The opposite happened. A crowd of more than 250,000 cheered her through the sunshine and streets of Glasgow, and there followed eleven

Her Majesty's coach party: on the second day of the Jubilee visit to Edinburgh, the Queen and Prince Philip rode in the Scottish State Coach to the General Assembly of the Church of Scotland

Royal appointment: while in Edinburgh, Her Majesty travelled to the Thistle Chapel of St Giles's Cathedral, where she installed Prince Charles as a Knight of the Most Noble Order of the Thistle

Thousands of people were at Holyrood Park on the slopes of Arthur's Seat when the Queen arrived to watch the Beating of Retreat. The army paid its own Jubilee tribute with a pomp and circumstance that set the audience singing and cheering

Jubilee treble: the Queen's visit to the General Assembly of the Church of Scotland is only the third she has made in her twenty-five years as Monarch

days of triumphant progress through Scotland's major cities. The only trouble, when it happened, was caused by *over*-enthusiasm.

In Glasgow, she drove in an open landau and attended a service in Glasgow Cathedral. She saw half a football match at Hampden Park, where a Glasgow select eleven beat an English select eleven 2-1, and in the evening went to a Royal Variety Performance at the King's Theatre. She was introduced to such well known non-Scots of the day as David Soul, an American gentleman currently appearing in a TV series called Starsky and Hutch, and an American Country and Western singing lady, Dolly Parton. At least Frankie Howerd, the English comedian, had the grace to wear the kilt, claiming he was half Scottish.

Next day in Govan she visited a council house where she was offered a cup of tea, but declined as she didn't have time. She went on to Perth, having spent the night on the Royal Train. A few Scottish Nationalists lined her route, occasionally chanting nationalistic slogans, but all in good humour. They were very fond of singing *Flower of Scotland*, which the SNP supporters had made their theme song that year, presuming it to be an ancient Highland lament, little knowing that it had been composed only four or five years ago.

The trouble happened in Dundee. During a walkabout in Camperdown Park, thousands of people broke through a flimsy rope barrier and swarmed around the Queen and Prince Philip, or the Duke of Edinburgh as he is always known in Scotland. Some elements of the crowd became hysterical, trampling and knocking each other over and cries could be heard of "I've touched the Queen." Her Majesty became separated from the Duke and for a moment she was in real physical danger. As all pop stars know, you can easily be maimed by overeager fans if you lose your protectors. However, the Queen was rescued and came to no harm.

The Duke was obviously touched by the scenes in Dundee and when a pub, the Windmill Bar, later sent him a poem, he replied also in verse. It verged between Betjeman and McGonagall, without reaching the heights of either, but it was gratefully received and framed by the pub:

> But the sight the most glorious in store for us to see,
> Was the friendly old Windmill in Hilltown, Dundee.

In Aberdeen, the Royal couple visited dockland and saw some of the latest technology helping to get oil for us all (not just for the Scot. Nats.) out of the North Sea. It was in Aberdeen thirty years previously that the Queen had undertaken her first public engagement when, as Princess Elizabeth, she'd opened a sailors' home.

The ceremonies in Edinburgh were more formal and regal than in Glasgow but the crowds were equally enthusiastic. The Prince of Wales joined the party and was installed as a Royal Knight of the Thistle in St Giles's Cathedral. Afterwards, the Prince was approached by a woman in the crowd opposite the cathedral who asked: "Give us a smile, Charlie." He was reported as replying: "What do you think I am bloody well doing?" Most papers omitted the bloody. As we all know, the Royal Family don't swear.

The Queen's tour of Scotland ended on May 26 with the obligatory garden party at the Palace of Holyrood House, where 9000 guests put on their best bonnets and tried to keep them on despite a strong wind. Glasgow was quietly pleased with the poor weather in Edinburgh – having laid on the sun when it was their turn. Then on May 27 the Queen flew back, after opening a new £10m terminal at Edinburgh Airport.

Scotland proved several things. The Scots still loved her dearly, despite rumours of creeping nationalism. During a visit to a meeting of the General Assembly of the Church of Scotland in Edinburgh, a lone voice had called out "Will ye no come back again?" At once, every man and woman in the crowded Assembly Hall started spontaneously singing.

The Scottish tour let people in London see that the Jubilee was creeping nearer. They'd taken little notice of the Commonwealth tour and were cool, if not to say rather cynical, about reports of crowd enthusiasm during those very unroyal-sounding walkabouts in strange-sounding foreign places. The manufacturers of bunting and Union Jacks, still working away, had begun to wonder if they might not make their fortunes after all. But the news from Scotland indicated that once the Queen came nearer home the crowds might start swarming.

Scotland also worried the police. On May 20, there were questions in the House of Commons about the over-enthusiastic crowds in Dundee and the danger to the Queen's safety. All over Britain, police and Special Branch officers started rechecking every procession and walkabout route which the Queen would use throughout the rest of Jubilee year, interviewing the residents of any likely buildings that might provide vantage points for terrorists. Scotland had caused pleasure – and worries.

Accent on youth: the Queen and Prince Philip drove in an open Land-Rover through thousands of people who had crowded into Annfield football ground, Stirling, for a youth pageant

CHAPTER THREE

Jubilee Eve – Waiting for Fireworks

On Monday, June 6, the eve of Jubilee Day, the Queen drove along the Long Walk to Windsor Great Park, escorted by thirty-six young people carrying torches. At 10 pm she lit the first in a chain of bonfires which by 11 pm had reached Saxavord in the Shetlands, the most northern point of the network of 102 beacons.

The first Queen Elizabeth in 1588 had had bonfires lit, some of them on exactly the same hills, to warn her people of the approach of the Spanish Armada. The second Queen Elizabeth was giving the signal that the Jubilee Week celebrations had at long last begun.

Throughout Britain, Lord-Lieutenants and other dignitaries set off their local bonfires. And having set off the first torch, the Queen lit another which was taken overnight by Jumbo jet to Sydney, to set off a chain of 3000 bonfires across Australia.

For most people, it was the bonfire ceremony that brought the Jubilee alive for the first time. Shops and streets seemed overnight to burst into red, white and blue. Offices and buildings put out more flags, though by now the Union Jack-makers had sold out. Those who delayed, not wishing to be openly chauvinistic, found there was now nothing left to buy.

The knockers were suddenly overtaken by events. The *New Statesman* devoted almost a whole issue to attacking the Jubilee. Its editor, Anthony Howard, returned from yet another broadcast in which he'd scoffed at the Jubilee idea to find that his office staff were putting up Jubilee bunting. Willie Hamilton, MP for Fife Central and an ardent anti-monarchist, said we'd all been brainwashed.

The Jubilee celebrations come alive: the Queen, accompanied by torch-carrying teenagers from many youth organisations, makes her way along the Long Walk to the Windsor beacon which, when lit, indicated the Jubilee proper had begun

---

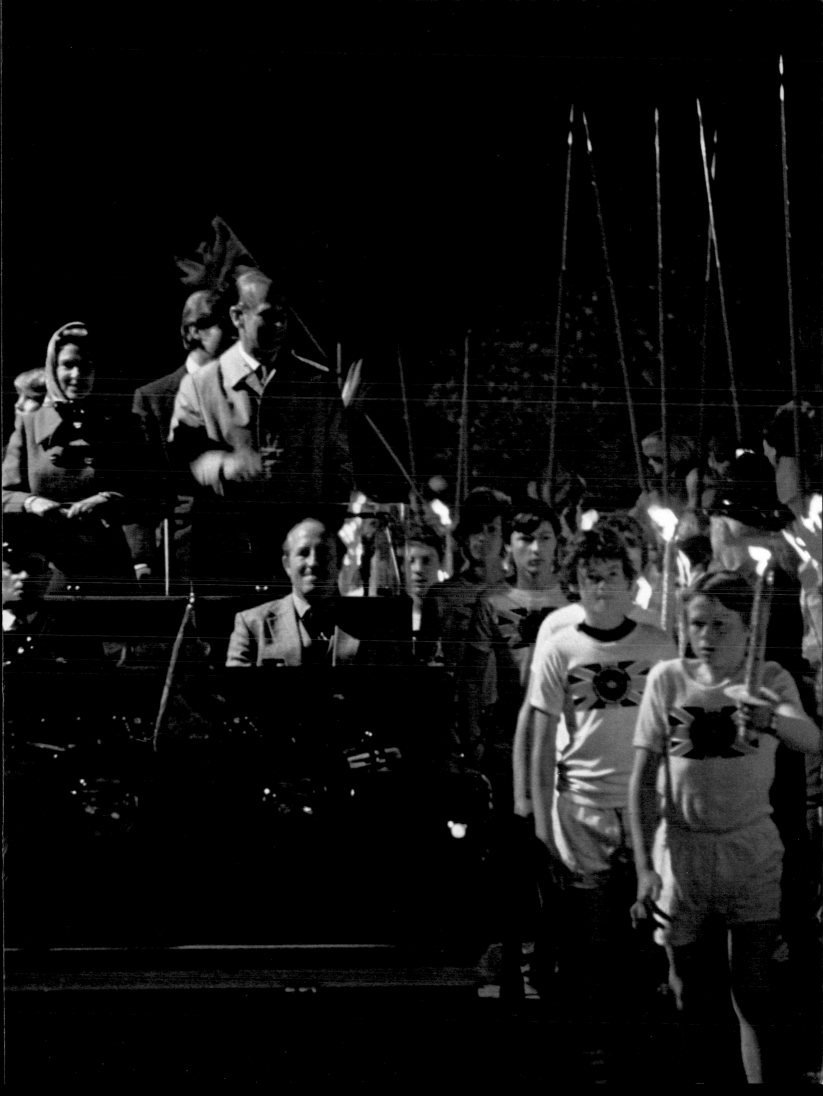

Overnight watchers
and early morning
risers: thousands of
eager Jubilee fans
camped overnight o
the streets of Londo
to lay claim to good
vantage points for t
Jubilee procession.
The grey dawn of
Jubilee Day itself
didn't dampen the
enthusiasm of those
who made the wait

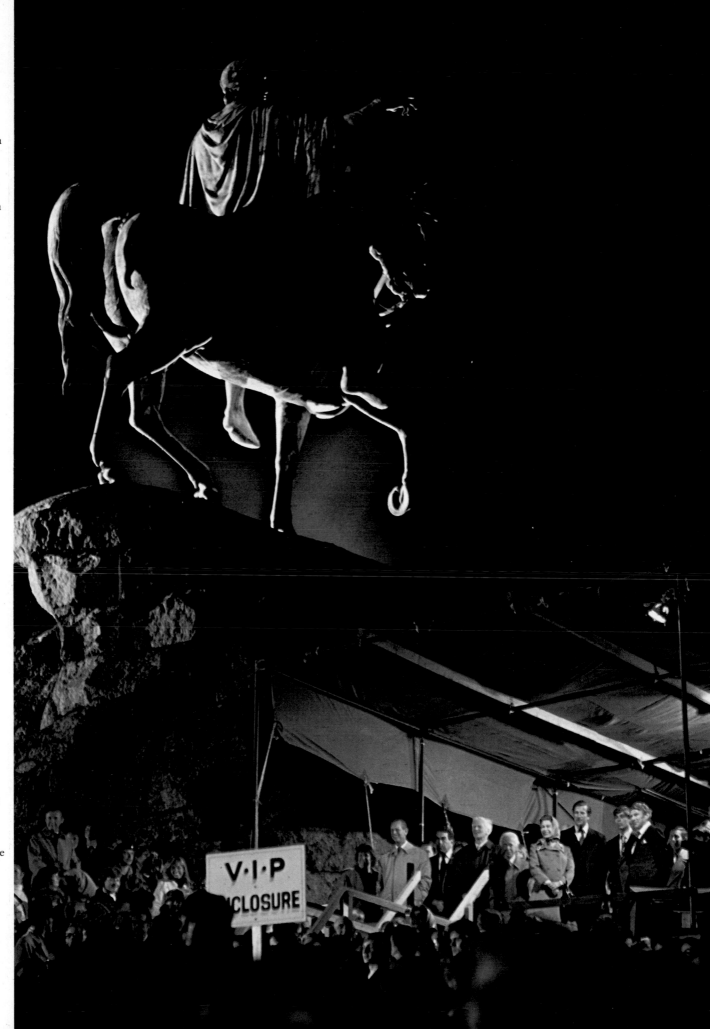

pontaneous com-
ustion: once the
ueen had lit the
Windsor beacon, it
as the signal for
onfires up and down
e country and
roughout the
ommonwealth to be
t alight. Firework
splays, too, went on
te into the night

he Royal Fireworks:
he Royal family and
uests admire and
njoy the fireworks
om the VIP enclosure
Windsor Park, in
e shadow of
e monument to
eorge III

V·I·P
ENCLOSURE

Jubilant fans: special hats, special flags, special messages, special coats, bags, hair-styles and even faces, were to be seen on Jubilee Day. Everyone joined in the happiness and jollity of the occasion, despite the grey skies

Shelter from the rain: just about anything was used for shelter on Jubilee Day. As on Coronation Day, the weather was rather grim

Although there had been showers in London during most of Monday, it did nothing to stop the steady stream of visitors from pouring in, some to gape at the decorations, some to gape at each other; many thousands came looking for somewhere to sleep the night, determined to get a good vantage point for the procession in the morning.

It was estimated that five million visitors had already arrived in London for Jubilee Day – two million of them from abroad and three million from outside London. Hotels and guest houses were overflowing and, as evening drew on, makeshift encampments were springing up on all pavements from the Mall to St Paul's. People produced sleeping bags, cooking-stoves, tested their cameras, waved Union Jacks at each other and then huddled good-humouredly together under umbrellas and plastic sheets hung from the crowd barriers, to avoid the next shower. Mums and dads who'd been brought as children to sleep overnight for the Coronation had brought their own children and tried to find the trees or the steps they'd used in 1953.

The police, unconcerned by even the possibility of anti-monarchist demonstrations, busied themselves with the traffic and with bedding the campers down for the night, very considerately pointing out which would be the noisy corners if people really did intend to sleep. Little choruses of *Land of Hope and Glory* could occasionally be heard over the noise of late-night traffic.

Messages of goodwill flooded into Buckingham Palace from all over the world at the rate of 1000 an hour. When the Royal family came back from Windsor around midnight, there were shouts of "We want the Queen" from the plastic huddles.

We want the Queen: thousands of happy Jubilee fans chant for the Queen and Royal family to come out on to the balcony of Buckingham Palace

CHAPTER FOUR

Jubilee Procession

The first coach left Buckingham Palace just after 10.25. It was a grey, rather overcast day, but the crowds cheered loyally and the band played the National Anthem, though only the first six bars. The first coach contained Princess Anne, recently announced as a mother-to-be, and her husband Mark Phillips. It was looked upon as the junior coach in the procession, hence the attenuated anthem. The full works were being reserved for the top-of-the-bill coach. The next five coaches contained other members of the Royal family. The Duchess of Kent, in coach number four, was also a mother-to-be, though it hadn't yet been announced.

The Queen Mother, in the seventh coach, received the full National Anthem. She was with her handsome young grandchildren, Prince Andrew and Prince Edward, and she received the loudest cheers so far. In 1937, when she was being crowned Queen Elizabeth, someone installed a decibel-counter along the route and that day it was Queen Mary with her pretty, young grandchildren, the princesses Elizabeth and Margaret Rose, who drew the loudest cheers.

Swaying out from under the centre arch of the Palace came the Golden Coach. Prince Philip was looking suitably regal and official in full ceremonial dress as Admiral of the Fleet, while beside him was the Queen, looking slightly apprehensive. Throughout the journey along jam-packed streets to St Paul's, Her Majesty continued to look serious and rather tense. Perhaps she'd had a bad night, what with all the cheering, camping crowds outside the Palace. Many had even climbed on the railings to shout, "We want the Queen." Lights had been seen from upstairs corridors and puzzled faces had stared out. Perhaps she wasn't looking forward to the journey. The Golden Coach is not exactly a

Where's the Queen? The long wait along the Jubilee procession route kept well-wishers on their toes for hours, but it was a wait rewarded by a split-second glimpse of the Golden Coach

luxury vehicle, however magnificent it looks from the outside. It was built in 1762 and had last been used for the Coronation. It weighs four tons and is noted for a bumpy ride.

Perhaps Her Majesty worried about the Big Day being an anti-climax. Preparations had been going on for well over a year, supervised by Sir Eric Penn, Comptroller of the Lord Chamberlain's Office since 1964 and once the front-man for the Lord Chamberlain in his role as stage censor. The Queen had been playing her own extensive and arduous Jubilee role for four long months, in front of several million people across the globe, and no doubt was very anxious that the Big Day should go well.

Perhaps it was simply the weather that made her look worried, upset on behalf of her loyal subjects who'd slept and waited in the rain and now looked like having some of the dazzle and glamour missing from their day. There was a section of the crowd who also looked a bit let down — disappointed by their first sight of their Jubilee Day Queen. How could she be a Queen without her crown and ermine and robes and jewels? Every window poster was showing her like that. Every child's drawing gave her at least a crown. Yet here she was, just an ordinary looking woman in a rose-pink coat and matching pink hat. And it wasn't even new! The experts immediately spotted where they'd seen that outfit before — when she'd been opening the Olympic Games in Canada the previous July.

It had been a last-minute, morning-of-the-day choice, so we learned later. She'd seen the dull dawn and decided to wear something bright and cheerful, something strong and glowing to brighten up all our colour photographs. It was a good choice. The pink certainly stood out, despite the rather suburban overtones. In the informal Seventies, why shouldn't she look relaxed and unregal? After all, despite the gaping millions, it was still a family affair. In a belt-tightening, hard economic time, it was more suitable to wear something unostentatious and old. She hadn't forgotten our monetary crisis while being fanned by Polynesian dancing girls and eating sucking pigs.

Unlike many of the watching millions, she understood what exactly was to come. She'd been doing her Jubilee walkabout for many months, though in far-off places, playing away matches which the natives at home had hardly noticed. Now it was the home game and she was going to introduce Londoners to the notion of a jolly walkabout. How could she possibly mingle with the fans if she was loaded down with tiaras and long trains?

The coach procession, the big, formal, regal part of the day, looked magnificent, the greatest pomp and pageantry that the world had seen for twenty-five years. And more than 500 million people in the outside world watched, their eyes glued to their TV sets. Royal-spotters everywhere had a field day.

Along the golden route: the Queen and Prince Philip, in the four-ton, 200-year-old Golden Coach, leave Buckingham Palace for the City of London and St Paul's for the Thanksgiving Service

The Royal carriages: *top*, Princess Margaret and Princess Alice with Viscount Linley and Lady Sarah Armstrong-Jones. *Below*, Queen Elizabeth the Queen Mother and Prince Charles on their return journey to Buckingham Palace after the St Paul's service

The fighting services: all sections of the serving forces were represented along the processional route to St Paul's, including a Naval guard of honour at Buckingham Palace, the Royal Air Force and Royal Marines' bandsmen

49

The first carriages of the family procession: *Above and left,* Prin« Anne and Capt. Mark Phillips; *top right,* Duke and Duchess of Kent and family; *bottom right,* Princess Margaret and Princess Alice.

Thousands of Royal cheers: the Queen, though obviously pensive about the ride in the Golden Coach, waves enthusiastically to all the jubilant people along The Mall

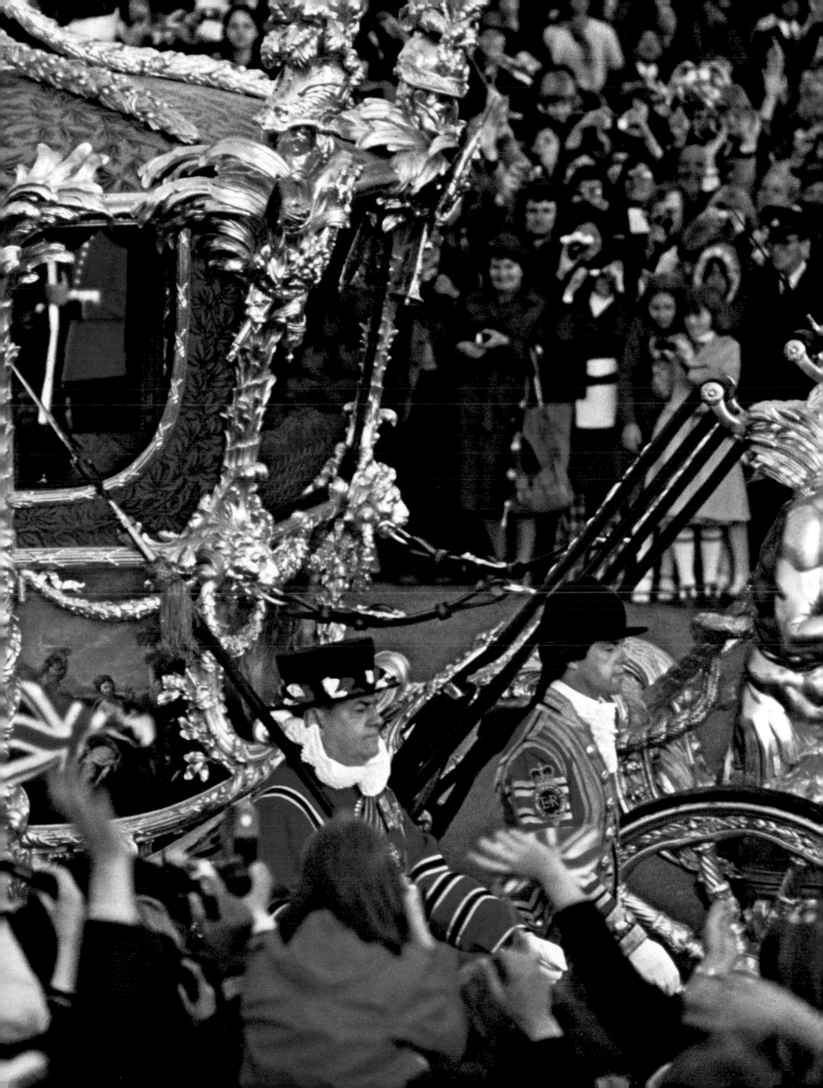

The Queen and Prince
Philip prepare to alight
from the Golden Coach
as it draws up before
St Paul's. The road
was heavily sanded to
prevent the horses
from slipping when
making tight turns on
the route

54

The Royal arrivals: the Lord Mayor of London greets the Queen and Prince Philip on their arrival at St Paul's, and leads them up the steps and into the Cathedral where nearly 2000 guests await the service of Thanksgiving

Ready for the
service: although
everyone knew
that the Queen and
Prince Philip were
going to St Paul's,
the cathedral itself
seemed unprepared
with a third of its
facade in
scaffolding

CHAPTER FIVE

St Paul's and the Walkabout

The Queen and Prince Philip arrived at St Paul's a little after 11.30. Everyone knew they were coming yet St Paul's seemed unprepared, with a third of its facade latticed in scaffolding. Workmen had not quite finished. Perhaps it will be clear for the Golden Jubilee.

Behind the Queen, on horseback, came Prince Charles. His horse, Centennial, had been presented only a few weeks previously by the Royal Canadian Mounted Police. A huge black gelding, it had undergone three years of intensive training since it was first chosen by the Queen in 1973. Many had missed Prince Charles, not realising who the figure was in the bearskin. He was dressed in the uniform of Colonel-in-Chief of the Welsh Guards and had to manoeuvre his jaw carefully, fearful of upsetting his bearskin. His extremely tight trousers made using a mounting block difficult when he got off his horse at St Paul's, and he appeared to be in some discomfort. During the ceremony itself his tight trousers made it impossible to kneel for the prayers. He admitted later that he had been very worried and was convinced he had stumbled – but watching himself on TV (action-replays being one of the wonders of the Queen's twenty-five years) he had been pleased to discover his stumble outside St Paul's hadn't shown.

The great West doors of St Paul's closed behind the Queen and Prince Philip, and the royal couple slowly made their way up the red carpeted nave, two solitary figures dwarfed by the magnificence of St Paul's. The congregation of 2700 stood to sing *All people that on earth do dwell*. The distinguished guests included the Royal family, leading members of the Government, a host of elderly bishops, ex-Prime Ministers such as Lord Home, Harold Macmillan, Edward Heath and Sir Harold Wilson, and Heads of the Commonwealth countries.

The Royal family sat both sides of the aisle in the front row. The Queen Mother, in autumn yellow, kept glancing proudly at her grandsons beside her. The Duchess of Kent was in bright leaf green and Princess Anne was in almond-green silk. Princess Margaret, like the Queen, wore a pink coat, but of a rather more tailored, more traditional style. Lord Snowdon, who had become officially separated from Princess Margaret some fifteen months earlier, was sitting eight rows behind. He leaned forward on his toes to catch sight of his children, Viscount Linley and Lady Sarah. Pierre Trudeau of Canada was just in front of him, another lonely figure. It was star-spotting time for all the millions watching round the world on television.

St Paul's was so brilliantly lit by the TV lights that everyone was able to have a really good look at the Queen, in long and constant close-ups. She did, most people agreed, look rather sad, standing very gravely beside Prince Philip. One commentator, Clive James of *The Observer*, was so bold as to state that she *had* looked "cheesed off", which immediately brought down the wrath of thousands of faithful Royal fans who will not allow one word of criticism.

An expert in deaf-and-dumb communication said later that he had lip-read what the Queen had said to the Prince during the service and it definitely seemed to him like "I feel sick." It must have been that coach. Whatever the reasons, her expression was suitably solemn for a solemn and suitably moving ceremony. The Archbishop of Canterbury, Dr Donald Coggan, spoke of the monarchy as something "at the heart of our national life of incalculable value – a spirit of devotion to duty and of service to others which has found its focus in a family and in a person." He also recalled how George VI and his beloved Queen "in days of war and post-war stress taught us afresh what duty means." There were tears in the eyes of the Queen Mother at these remarks, and although she bravely bit her bottom lip she could scarcely contain them.

Once St Paul's had disgorged its distinguished visitors, the mood immediately changed. The congregation poured out with beaming faces, funny hats, turning and staring,

nodding and smiling, a colourful and exotic collection of the very important, all in their best and fanciest clothes. The Queen and Prince Philip were off first, setting such a cracking pace that her personal attendants, the members of the Royal Household, could scarcely keep up. Her Private Secretary, Sir Martin Charteris, got himself entangled with his sword as he tried to take pinches of his beloved snuff. The Royal party seemed well pleased to be out of St Paul's and back with the people. And their smiles showed it.

There were spontaneous bursts of cheering as the Queen started her walkabout, both she and Prince Philip darting forward to talk to people in the crowds. The pink bells on the green stalks on the Queen's hat bobbed about furiously as she threw back her head and laughed loudly. She was full of solicitous remarks. "Oh dear, did you get awfully wet? Are you frozen?" A student asked her if she had a mechanical arm inside her coat to help her with all the waving. "Oh no," said the Queen. "I haven't reached that stage yet." Small children presented her with posies, despite the worried looks of security men, and everyone tried to take their own special Queenly photographs. She dealt with them magnificently, going out of her way to smile and stay still for a few seconds, particularly if a young photographer caught her eye – as in the cover photograph of this book. Prince Philip received lots of shouts of "Hello Darling" from some cockney ladies, knowing he'd enjoy a bit of cheek, and he was suitably witty in reply. One small boy ran forward and tried to get the Queen's autograph but he was gently refused by an equerry who explained, "She only signs Acts of Parliament."

The Queen was with the Lord Mayor of London and his Lady Mayoress as they strolled down Cheapside. "How happy they all look," she exclaimed. Her universal popularity was apparent to all, a level of affection which it had taken Queen Victoria fifty years to achieve.

The walk from St Paul's to the Guildhall was scheduled to last only twenty minutes, but it took twice as long as the Queen stopped to chat and beam. "Everyone quite happy," she asked another group, then replied to her own question. "I am. What a lovely day. We are so lucky."

Opposite: The Royal procession: as the Queen and Prince Philip make their way up the aisle of St Paul's, the great West doors are closed and a hush falls on the people gathered beneath the great dome

Below: The congregation: the Royal family and many heads of state were among the hundreds of honoured guests specially invited to the service

Top left: Princess Anne (mother-to-be) and husband Captain Mark Phillips, with Princess Alice. *Below:* the Queen and Prince Philip

The Queen and Prince Philip before the congregation of St Paul's, which
included four past Prime Ministers of Great Britain

The heart of the
nation: the
Archbishop of
Canterbury, Dr
Donald Coggan, in
his address, said
that the monarchy
was of incalculable
value to the nation

Below the dome of
St Paul's: the
Queen and Prince
Philip before the
congregation

Top left: Princess Margaret, Princess Anne, Captain Mark Phillips, Princess Alice, the Duchess and Duke of Gloucester. *Top right:* the Queen Mother and Prince Charles leaving St Paul's at the end of the service followed (*below*) by some of the many guests

The Jubilee walkabout: in complete contrast to the seriousness of the St Paul's service, the Queen and Prince Philip laughed, smiled and chatted their way through Cheapside to the Guildhall for lunch

What a lovely day: as the Queen continued her walk through Cheapside she was heard to say over and over again "Isn't it a lovely day." They were words echoed by all the onlookers lucky enough to talk with the Queen

Smile please: there was little need for this enthusiastic amateur photographer to ask the Queen to say "Cheese". Throughout the forty-minute walk to the Guildhall the Queen was very happy and relaxed

CHAPTER SIX

Guildhall

There were 650 guests at the Guildhall, including Commonwealth leaders in London for the Commonwealth conference, and they ate a three-course lunch of salmon trout, fillet of Angus beef, followed by Charentais melon; all very sensible, after all the excitement.

The Lord Mayor of London, Sir Robin Gillet, the Queen's host, recalled the day King George VI reviewed a cadet force at the Nautical College, Pangbourne, in 1943.

I have a photograph of that occasion; it is always with me. The Queen, aged seventeen years and two months, was accompanied by her father. I was the right marker cadet at the rear, aged seventeen years and seven months. Never did I dream thirty-four years later I would carry the sword of my city before my Sovereign at that girl's Silver Jubilee service.

The Queen was very impressed, though she was frequently trying to keep an eye on thirteen-year-old Prince Edward, to see how he was getting on with his lunch further down the table. He sat upright, his hair shining as if his mother had brushed it, next to Mrs Callaghan, the Prime Minister's wife. He appeared to be having a good tuck-in, and looked pink-cheeked and rather excited. Prince Andrew, aged seventeen, was beautifully composed and photogenic, well used to having the cameras, and the girls, admiring his handsome looks. He sat up confidently and talked quietly to the Prime Minister. Princess Anne was next to Archbishop Makarios, but didn't appear to say much to him. Princess Margaret and Earl Mountbatten talked constantly together, the white locks of his hair almost becoming entwined with the flowers on the brim of the Princess's shocking-pink hat.

The Queen made a speech in reply to the Lord Mayor, and to her people everywhere, talking mainly about the Commonwealth and its values today. "At the Silver Jubilee of 1935 and at my Coronation, the Empire and the Commonwealth came to London; this time the travelling is in both directions and I think we can claim to be doing our fair share." She concluded with two sentences which were picked out and passed on by every newspaper the next day. "My Lord Mayor, when I was twenty-one I pledged my life to the service of our people and I asked for God's help to make good that vow. Although that vow was made in my salad days, when I was green in judgment, I do not regret nor retract one word of it."

All the way back to the Palace, the crowds roared their approval, thanking the Queen for her twenty-five years of devotion to those vows. She and the Prince returned in an open landau, the Golden Coach having been put back into storage until who knows when, who knows why.

At least 100,000 people were jammed outside Buckingham Palace, squeezing round the statue of Queen Victoria and up the Mall, booming and chanting, "We want the Queen." As with the 1953 Coronation, the Queen and Prince Philip waved from the balcony, being joined later by the rest of the Royal family. In all, they made three appearances, three appearances captured a million times by loyal cameras.

The British love a Royal line-up, a final balcony appearance, the end to a perfect Royal day. It is a scene which as children we were allowed to look at in old Jubilee books on rainy days, or when ill in bed and in need of something not too strenuous or taxing, to turn over and be made to feel good again. It goes into the mind and the memory, and we grow up believing we actually did see George VI and the young Princesses, giving similar waves from that same balcony. Or was it even earlier Royals? Millions who were not there that day, on June 7, 1977, when the Queen and Prince Philip gave their traditional waves, will believe they saw it in the flesh, taking personal possession of that familiar image. It was more than just the end of a perfect day, perfect but for a few showers. It was the end of a perfect twenty-five years of dutiful and loyal devotion by our Queen.

The Guildhall lunch: the Queen spoke mainly about the Commonwealth and its values today, concluding with the fact that at twenty-one she had pledged her life to the service of the people of Great Britain and the Commonwealth. ''Although that vow was made in my salad days, when I was green in judgment, I do not regret nor retract one word of it.'' The Queen was speaking in reply to a speech made by the Lord Mayor of London, Sir Robin Gillet

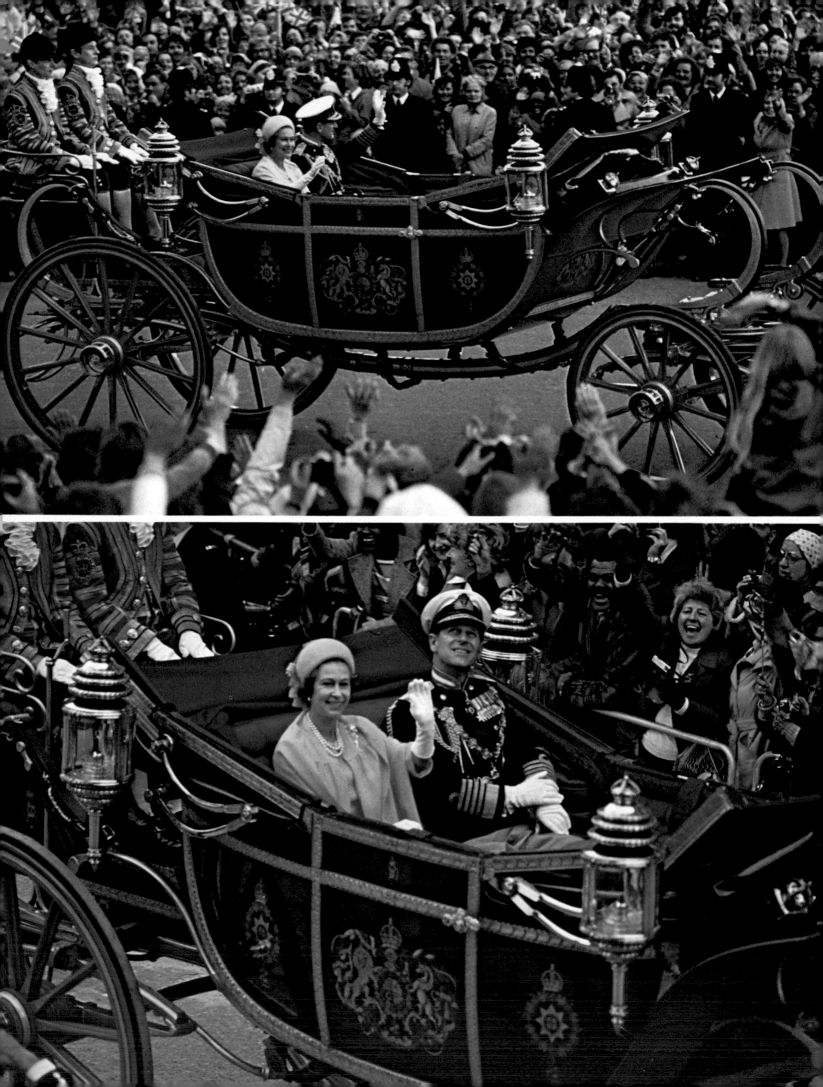

Homeward bound: at the conclusion of the Guildhall lunch, the Queen and Prince Philip rode on an open landau back to Buckingham Palace, acknowledging the cheers from the crowds along the route. Once back at the Palace an enormous crowd of more than 100,000 people gathered in front of the Palace railings and roared for the Royal family to come out on to the balcony

CHAPTER SEVEN

Street Parties and Decorations

It was the first time since the war that so many people had come out into the streets and met so many other people. It all began slowly and quietly, like most of the Jubilee preparations, with the collectors worrying if they would get enough donations to buy the children Jubilee mugs and whether the stuck-up woman at number 11 would really cut all those sandwiches as she'd promised. Bunting was one of the big problems: even when the whip-rounds had produced enough money, if you waited until the last moment there was none left to buy.

Shops spent a fortune decorating themselves, and the most apparently unroyal places managed to shove up a picture of Her Gracious Majesty, from funeral parlours to sex shops. In Oxford Street, London, they spent £250,000 promoting the Jubilee – but as trade went up by 40 per cent during the Jubilee period, they more than got their money back.

Local councils refused to subsidise street parties, which turned out to be a challenge as neighbours got together to compete with other streets to put on the best show. Havering in Essex maintained afterwards that it had more street parties than any other Borough in the land – 492 they managed, out of a total of just 1600 streets. They gave a prize for the best street to Rectory Gardens and The Meads in Upminster, which was decorated like a castle's battlements, with silver cannons and roses in each hedge of the eighty houses.

Britain's immigrant population joined in, with the Chinese producing Jubilee dragons, and the West Indians providing Jubilee steel-band music. There were a lot of native Morris Men in the Midlands. At Durham prison, thirty-five women prisoners in the top security wing pooled their earnings for a Jubilee supper. The wing was decorated "as festive as any street party", said an official. They also had a sports meeting with a Jubilee mug for the winner.

Decorations fit for the Queen: Jubilee decorations had been slow to appear early in the year, but once the Queen had lit the Jubilee beacon at Windsor it fired everyone up and down the country to join in the mood of the occasion, and traders' dreams of swift business were more than realised

---

In the Jubilee mood: almost every household had an original idea on how the Jubilee message of congratulations should be expressed

Supporting roles: even manufacturers of ladies' underwear produced special editions of garments for the Jubilee. Street parties, too, had their own styles and flair; milkmen joined in the fun, and for the children there were Jubilee train-rides accompanied by some very attractive attendants. For the souvenir hunters, there were all things bright and beautiful

Three cheers for the Queen: smile, please, for the Jubilee
camera. Boroughs up and down the country enjoyed themselves on a scale unseen since the end of the war

Along the Jubilee road: on Jubilee day many roads were closed to traffic. Communities who had collected money throughout the year set up street parties for children. Sandwiches, buns, cream cake, ice-cream and pop were top of the menu for the children; there was also tea and sandwiches for the mums and dads, and a selection of stronger tipples for those with hardier constitutions

What dainty dishes to set before the Queen: not only food, but even pets took on the red, white and blue of the Jubilee spirit. In country or city, whether with bunnies or bunting, everyone was caught up in jubilant mood

All the fun of the party: for once in twenty-five rather difficult years everyone joined in the celebrations. Little girls were elected local Jubilee queens, and policemen swapped pints with revellers

For the Queen and country: it wasn't only cities, towns and boroughs that captured the spirit of the occasion; international communities joined in the Jubilee fun as well. In Regent Street, London, the Hong Kong community paraded a fearsome but nevertheless Jubilee-spirited dragon

CHAPTER EIGHT

VIPs

The Queen entertained the Commonwealth leaders during Jubilee Week, all of them assembled for several days in London for their Conference. When she first gave a banquet for her Commonwealth PMs at Buckingham Palace twenty-five years ago, the Commonwealth consisted of only eight members – the big white five (Britain, Australia, Canada, New Zealand and South Africa) and three brown ones (India, Pakistan and Ceylon.) This time the Queen presided over thirty-five Commonwealth heads of government, the vast majority of them black.

It was a most impressive line-up, even more impressive when one considers the political upheavals and rearrangements of the past twenty-five years. It was still the world's biggest family of countries. The leaders represented 1000 million people, a quarter of the world's population.

President Kenneth Kaunda of Zambia paid a remarkable tribute to the Queen and the "People's Commonwealth", saying that the Queen's Silver Jubilee was a "unique event" in human history.

Ever since God made man, no reigning British monarch on these islands has had such a large number of leaders of so many millions of free people joining in this happy and historical occasion. Our presence in London during the celebrations is the product of British wisdom in those twenty-five crucial years.

Luckily, saving the embarrassment of everyone, President Amin of Uganda didn't turn up, despite hints that he still might. The previous Sunday, *The Sunday Times* had revealed the flight to London of one of his Ministers, who had described in great detail the murders and outrages being carried out in Uganda.

Mr Callaghan laid on a surprise flight up to Gleneagles in Scotland, where twenty-seven Commonwealth statesmen, plus wives and escorts, naturally hoped to get in some golf, but the weather was too bad. However, Mr Trudeau and Lee Kuan Yew of Singapore did get in some swimming, in the hotel's indoor swimming pool.

President Jimmy Carter of the United States didn't make the Jubilee Week ceremonies – instead he sent his son James Earl III, better known as Chip – but then he had met the Queen earlier in her Jubilee year.

He had arrived in London on May 5 to confer with Western leaders at the Downing Street summit. "I am very proud to come to Great Britain", said Mr Carter at the airport, "as the first country outside my own nation as President of the United States." He went up to the North-East for a whistle-stop tour, trailing hordes of security men, assistants and the Press with him. He flattered the Geordies by managing to pronounce 'Howay the lads', the rallying cry of Newcastle United football fans. He planted a tree in Washington, County Durham, to commemorate the original home of George Washington's family, but alas it died. It was a tulip tree, brought with the President on his plane, and it was admitted later that it had died *en route*. Not wishing to disappoint the Geordie crowds, he had gone ahead and done the tree-planting ceremony as planned, shovelling in twelve big spadefuls. It was a very good performance. So were his earnest wishes for a continuation of the old and special relations between Britain and the USA.

The Queen gave the President and other Western leaders dinner at Buckingham Palace on the night of Saturday, May 7. President Carter sat between the Queen and Princess Margaret, relaxed and at ease, confirming his big success in the public relations stakes of the previous few days. Earlier, on leaving Number 10, he said he was behaving "just like any other little old world leader". Also present were Giscard d'Estaing from France and Helmut

The Commonwealth
family: before the Jubilee
celebrations began, the
Queen met the heads of
the family of nations that
makes up the Common-
wealth in the Music Room
at Buckingham Palace.
*From left to right, front
row:* Dr Hastings Banda
(Malawi); Morarji Desai
(India); Malcolm Fraser
(Australia); Michael
Manley (Jamaica); the late
President Makarios
(Cyprus); Mr Callaghan;
Kenneth Kaunda (Zambia);
General Ziaur Rahman
(Bangladesh); Robert
Muldoon (New Zealand);
Brigadier Shehu Yar'Adua
(Nigeria).
Second row: Michael
Somare (Papua–New
Guinea); Siaka Stevens
(Sierra Leone); Sir
Seewoosagur Ramgoolam
(Maritius); J. M. G. M.
Adams (Barbados); Sir
Eric Gairy (Grenada);
Aboud Jumbe (Tanzania);
General F. W. K. Akuffo
(Ghana); Lynden Pindling
(Bahamas); Prince
Tu'ipelechake (Tonga).
Back row: Taisi Tupuola
(Western Samoa); Datuk
Hussein Bin Onn
(Malaysia); Sir Kamisese
Mara (Fiji); Dr Leabua
Jonathan (Lesotho); Vice-
President D. T. Arap Moy
(Kenya); Lee Kuan Yew
(Singapore); Dom Mintoff
(Malta); Fred Wills
(Guyana); Col. Mapheru
Dlamini (Swaziland); John
Donaldson (Trinidad and
Tobago); Sir Dawd Jawara
(Gambia); Sir Seretse
Khama (Botswana); Pierre
Trudeau (Canada).

93

Schmidt from West Germany. It made an historic photograph, though technically the only ones taken were a bit thin and colourless. Next morning, President Carter got up early and went for 8 o'clock Communion Service at Westminster Abbey, where he complained to the Archdeacon of Westminster, during a tour of the Abbey, that Dylan Thomas was not commemorated in Poets' Corner. Mr Carter is one of those who thinks that Dylan Thomas was one of the twentieth century's greatest poets.

At the end of Jubilee Week, there were more formal gatherings with the annual Trooping the Colour ceremony on Horse Guards Parade. For the third time in five days, the Queen made her way down the Mall between massive crowds, this time riding side-saddle on her horse, Burmese. She was dressed as Colonel-in-Chief of the Scots Guards whose colour was being trooped, accompanied by Prince Philip, Prince Charles and other members of the Royal Family, all wearing their uniforms.

The Downing Street summit: *left to right*: the Queen with Pierre Trudeau, Canada; M. Takeo Miki, the Japanese Premier; Princess Margaret, Prime Minister James Callaghan, Prince Charles, President Giscard d'Estaing of France, Her Majesty the Queen Mother, President Carter of the US, Prime Minister Giulio Andreotti of Italy, Prince Philip, and Chancellor of Germany Helmut Schmidt. The reception was held in the Blue Drawing Room of Buckingham Palace

The Queen's Official Birthday: Her Majesty the Queen takes the salute at the Trooping the Colour ceremony. *Overleaf:* The Queen with Prince Philip and Prince Charles attending the ceremony of Trooping the Colour

CHAPTER NINE

River Procession

One of the Queen's longest days during Jubilee was the river procession and associated festivities on Thursday, June 9, which started at 10.30 in the morning and didn't finish till after 11 at night, more than twelve hours of non-stop handshaking, waving, chatting, receiving bouquets and being introduced to several hundred dignitaries.

First stop for the Queen was Greenwich, where she met some Scouts and local children. Then she went on board the Royal launch *Nore*, being piped aboard by cadets of the nearby Royal Naval College and welcomed by her scarlet-liveried watermen. Prince Philip was with her. One of his many titles is Baron Greenwich. They made a stop at Deptford, where the first Elizabeth knighted Francis Drake. There had been a panic three hours earlier when a newly-fixed platform to Deptford Wharf was found to be three feet under water – together with a vast expanse of red carpet. It was replaced just in time by red lino, quickly lifted from a nearby office.

Throughout their river trip, the Royal couple were followed by scores of gaily decorated barges and small boats, including a flotilla of twenty-three of the Thames ''little ships'' which took part in the evacuation of Dunkirk in 1940. There was also a three-mile-long river pageant later on, which the Queen watched from County Hall, the headquarters of the Greater London Council. She arrived for tea with the Archbishop of Canterbury at Lambeth Palace, and reviewed the assembled men and machines of the London Fire Brigade at its riverside headquarters.

The Queen changed in the evening, from a powder-blue coat and sailor-style hat into a yellow wool coat and spotted turban hat, and watched a fireworks display from the roof of the Shell building. Suitable water music was played over the public address system and more than 750,000 people watched the display. ''I would like to emphasise that the behaviour of the crowd was absolutely perfect,'' said James Kennedy, Chief Officer of the GLC Parks Department.

The Queen's Jubilee River Pageant: on Thursday, June 9 in Jubilee Week the Queen boarded the Royal launch *Nore* at Greenwich for what was officially called Her Majesty the Queen's River Progress. It was to be one of the longest days in the Jubilee for Her Majesty

Down in Dockland: the river trip included many stops so that the Queen could go ashore and meet local people. There was plenty of cheering, hand-shaking and the amateur photographers had a field day snapping Royal pictures

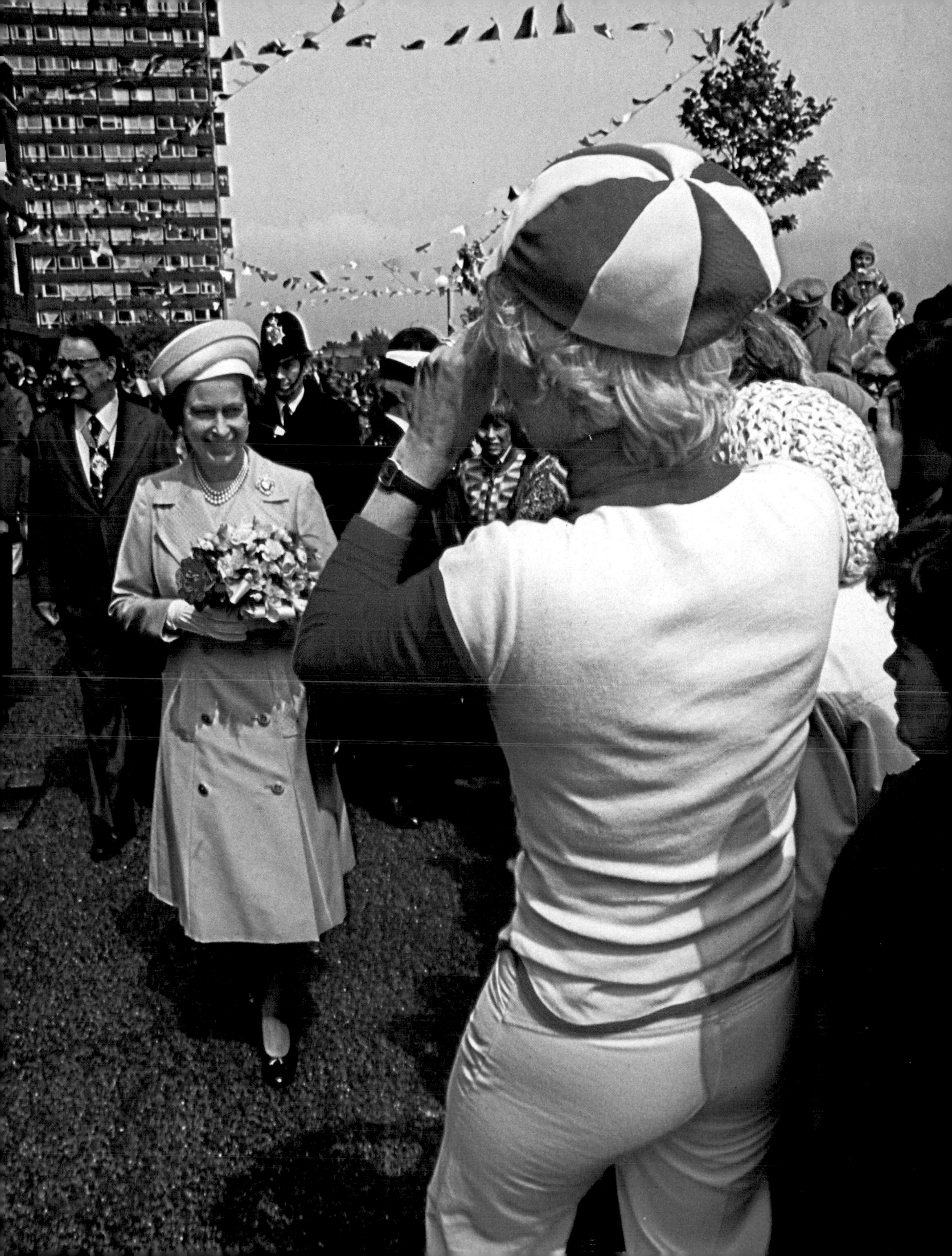

Down on old Father
Thames: thousands of
people crowded the banks
of the river to see the
Queen. Many disregarded
safety warnings and
crowded on to the river
craft for a better view of
the Queen and Prince
Philip. One of the most
picturesque vantage points
was from the old Thames
sailing barges

105

Queen of the riverfront: old and young people welcomed the Queen along the river route. It was in complete contrast to the formality of the journey to St Paul's

Lunch by Royal agreement: the Queen's watermen who manned the Royal launch *Nore* take their lunch-break of beer and sandwiches. The river trip was a long day for these men as well. Despite the rain, one of the stops the Queen made at Lambeth was to inspect members of the London Fire Brigade

Royal fireworks: after spending a very full day on the river, the Queen was the guest of honour at the River Thames Jubilee Fireworks display which she watched from the rooftop of the Shell building. The Royal party returned to Buckingham Palace only to be faced by an enormous crowd chanting for the Royal family to appear on the balcony. The crowd's insistence was duly answered shortly after midnight

CHAPTER TEN

Royal Children

The Royal children had a jolly year. They were particularly in evidence during Jubilee Week, looking clean and shiny in their respective Royal coaches, their faces well scrubbed and their hair gleaming, being admired openly by the Queen Mother or worried about quietly by their parents. It was nice that during the year a new generation of Royals should arrive on the scene – in the summer it was announced that Princess Anne, the Duchess of Kent and the Duchess of Gloucester were each going to give birth in the autumn.

The Queen's two elder children, Prince Charles and Princess Anne, do not count as children any more, and even the other two looked very grown up. Prince Andrew was seventeen during the year (on February 19) and Prince Edward had his thirteenth birthday on March 10.

Prince Andrew is the one most likely to keep the gossip columns happy for many years to come. Very early on he was nicknamed the "Clown Prince" after reports that he'd kicked a football through a greenhouse at Windsor; fused the lights at Sandringham; taken Prince Charles's Aston Martin for a spin in the grounds of Balmoral; put detergent into the Windsor swimming pool; and generally made free with the whoopee cushions. He's taller than Prince Charles, close to six feet tall and broad shouldered with it. At Gordonstoun he was known by some as 'The Sniggerer' because his opening conversational gambit tended to be, "Have you heard the one about . . ."

This year he was at school in Canada for two terms, at Lakefield College, a hundred miles north of Toronto, and made a big hit with the Canadian Press, and with young Canadian girls. He made a deal on one occasion with his detective so he could go out alone dancing with a Canadian girl. Another time he went fishing – alone in a boat with a girl and a bowl of cherries. During his stay in Canada, girls were seen to be wearing T-shirts emblazoned with Randy Andy, Andy for King or I'm an Andrew Windsor girl.

Prince Edward had a much quieter year, contenting himself by playing with his cousins, Lady Sarah Armstrong-Jones and Viscount Linley. He was still at Heatherdown prep school in Berkshire, but was due to go to Gordonstoun. His main school interests were photography and soccer, but he was better at cricket according to one of his teachers. "In football, like lots of little boys, Prince Edward rushes about for five minutes, and then does nothing." During the early part of the year he went with the school on a two-week package tour – ski-ing in the Italian Alps. Even on the ski-slopes, the inevitable detective was right behind. (In Italy, kidnapping children of wealthy parents was a growth industry that year.)

Princess Margaret's two children were spotted by everybody during the St Paul's ceremony, especially as they were eight rows away from their father, Lord Snowdon. Viscount Linley became sixteen in November, while Lady Sarah Armstrong-Jones was thirteen in May. Both were at the co-ed boarding school Bedales.

The Duke of Gloucester was at most Jubilee Week ceremonies with his Danish-born wife, Birgitte. Not much was seen of their son, the Earl of Ulster, but then he was only two years old – three in October.

The Duke of Kent's three children were seen quite often – the Earl of St Andrews, aged fifteen, Lord Nicholas Windsor, aged seven, and Lady Helen Windsor, aged thirteen. The Earl of St Andrews sounds academically the cleverest of the young Royals. He won a scholarship to Eton from Heatherdown prep school, the first member of the Royal Family to become a King's Scholar, living in the oldest part of the school.

For some reason, not many photographs appeared of Princess Alexandra and her family during Jubilee Day – their coach passed too quickly and the photographers were busy spotting elsewhere. But her two children were with her, James, aged thirteen, and Marina, aged eleven.

The Royal children: children of the Royal family were much in evidence during the Jubilee celebrations. Prince Andrew, here, proved to be one of the most popular, not only with the mums and dads but with the young ladies

The new generation of Royals: during the year the Press captured Prince Andrew with one of his girlfriends, Sandy Jones. Prince Edward and Viscount Linley showed themselves to be good friends, while Lady Sarah Armstrong-Jones proved that she was at home with the hounds. Prince Edward, too, showed lots of enthusiasm at Badminton

Younger members of the Royal family: the service at St Paul's proved a little too long for Lord Nicholas Windsor, who found it difficult to hold back a yawn. With him are, from the left, the Earl of St Andrews, Lady Helen Windsor, the Duchess of Kent, the Duke of Kent and Lady Sarah Armstrong-Jones. *Right*, the young Alexander, Earl of Ulster, gets a shoulder-ride from his father, the Duke of Gloucester

St Paul's and members of the Royal family: *from right to left* – James Ogilvy, the Hon. Angus Ogilvy, Princess Alexandra, Marina Ogilvy, Prince Michael; *front* – George, Earl of St Andrews, the Duchess of Kent, Lord Nicholas Windsor, Lady Helen Windsor and the Duke of Kent

CHAPTER ELEVEN

Provincial Tour

The Queen had hardly recovered from the rigours and excitements of Jubilee Week before she was on tour once more, this time round other parts of the British Isles. In late June she did an extensive tour of the North-West of England, taking in Manchester and Lancashire, and then on to a three-day tour of Wales, meeting up with the Royal Yacht *Britannia* once more. It's a wonder they didn't miss each other at least once. All year, the Queen and *Britannia* chased each other round the globe, playing hide-and-seek up estuaries, down rivers, across oceans, but they still managed to coincide at the right place at the right time.

In Wales, the Queen and the Prince walked round Harlech Castle, one of the garrison points established by Edward I to complete his mastery of the Welsh. Several demonstrators, still worried about English domination, distributed banners and anti-royalist leaflets, but the Queen seemed unaware of any protest.

In Blaenau Festiniog, a scrap dealer, carrying a four-ton load of old iron and his grandmother, unwittingly got caught up in the Royal procession. Thinking the procession had passed he had pulled into the road, but found he was part of the cavalcade and couldn't get out for three miles. "I reckon I got more cheers from the crowd than the Queen," he said afterwards.

In July, the Queen toured the Greater London boroughs she hadn't so far visited and then went to East Anglia, Humberside, Yorkshire, the North-East and the Midlands. In August she visited the West Country.

Many people had warned against her two-day visit to Northern Ireland. At one time it looked in danger of being cancelled. However, the first half of the year had proved slightly better than the year before. There had been no explosions in London since the Oxford Street incidents in January. The killings and bombs and violence had continued in Northern Ireland, but not on such a scale as the previous year. In the first half of the year, 80 people had died in Ulster compared with 150 in the six months of the previous year.

During Jubilee Week itself, there had been bunting and decorations in shops throughout Ulster, though there had been some disagreement in Londonderry on the form of a Jubilee greetings telegram to be sent to the Queen. The council had originally proposed the wording: "We, the loyal subjects of Her Majesty the Queen in Londonderry..." After protests from the non-loyalists, this was changed to: "We, the undersigned loyalist councillors." After further arguments, the telegram idea was dropped.

The Queen's visit to Northern Ireland happened during what is not usually a happy week in the Province. It fell between the anniversary of the start of internment and the annual march of the Londonderry Apprentice Boys. So the Queen and Prince Philip found themselves at the heart of one of the biggest security operations ever mounted.

For the first time in her life, Her Majesty was obliged to fly by helicopter after advice from her security men. They said it was the only way they could guarantee her safety. The Queen wasn't keen because as everybody knows she just doesn't like helicopters, unlike her husband and eldest son. She landed safely in the grounds of eighteenth-century Hillsborough Castle, fourteen miles from Belfast – and another fact could be entered into everyone's Royal history books. She emerged from the big, red, shiny bird of the Queen's Flight wearing a most appropriate emerald-green outfit. She looked relieved, but a trifle tired.

In all, nearly 32,500 police, soldiers and security men were detailed to look after the Royal couple's safety. On the first day, Prince Philip piloted his own helicopter to a Belfast shipyard, where he had a jovial time meeting the men. The Queen was greeted by local schoolchildren. In the evening, there was a reception on board *Britannia* for security-cleared local dignitaries. The Queen and Prince Philip never slept on Ulster soil, again because of the security risk, and instead the Royal couple had full board aboard *Britannia*. On the second day, the Queen and Prince Philip visited the new University of Ulster at Coleraine. But again, as on the previous day, there were no car or coach processions; and there were no public walkabouts to meet local people.

Despite the chilling threat of the terrorists, the Queen's determination to include Ulster in her Jubilee year won her many friends and admirers from Loyalists and Republicans, Catholics and Protestants alike, and everyone gave a huge sigh of relief when it all safely came to an end.

he Royal tour of the
rovinces: the Queen and
rince Philip had hardly
ecovered from the rigours
f Jubilee Week before they
et off on a tour of the
ritish Isles. *Right*: the
oyal couple meet the cast
f TV's Coronation Street in
1anchester, and, *below*,
njoy a display of gymnastics
y Stockport schoolchildren

Queen and country: after the tour of North
West England, the Queen then proceeded t
Wales where she embarked on a three-day
tour. *Top:* St Helens, Lancashire; *centre*
Portsmouth; *bottom:* Cardiff; *right:* the walk
about in Dyfed, Wales

verpool's Majesty: the Queen drove through Liverpool
an open Range Rover, and she is pictured here with
e Roman Catholic Metropolitan Cathedral in the back-
ound as she makes her way to the Anglican Cathedral.
uring her day in the city 17,000 schoolchildren
esented a musical pageant

l the fun of the fair: during the Silver Jubilee two-day
ur of South Humberside the Royal couple visited
igg, *top*, to watch a musical pageant. Nine-year-old
el Garratt, in the foreground, designed the cover for
e day's special Jubilee programme, and with him is
ark Phillips (no relation) who composed a special poem.
ntre: the Queen at Durham Town Hall. *Bottom:* in
ewcastle

Out and about: *top* – the Queen in Ipswich; *centre*, meeting the people of Leeds; *bottom*, arriving at Hillsborough Castle near Belfast after her first flight by helicopter, the Queen commences her historic visit to Northern Ireland; *right*, the Royal walkabout in York

CHAPTER TWELVE

The Royal
Naval Review
at Spithead

British fleets have been having themselves reviewed by the Monarchy at Spithead for centuries. Edward III in 1346 cast his eye over more than a thousand of his ships. George III was rowed out in a barge when it was his turn in 1773, though he had only twenty-five ships in all to inspect. In 1914, the line stretched for forty miles. In 1953 the Queen saw about two hundred warships at her Coronation Review. This year, for her Jubilee Review, she saw just over one hundred. Such Royal Reviews are reserved these days for Coronations and Jubilees – so who knows when the next one will be. Who knows if there will even be a Navy at the next Jubilee.

However, the British fleet is still the third largest in the world, after the USA and Russia, and it put on a magnificent show despite the dull weather. Low cloud reduced the number of helicopters from 110 to 70, and the appearance of 40 Naval Phantom fighters and other planes had to be cancelled. *The Sunday Times Magazine* had hired a helicopter at wild expense (£600 for five hours), as it had done for Jubilee Week, but the poor weather played havoc with the photographs. The aerial shot of *Britannia*, sailing up between the lines of massive warships, is a rather stunning photograph, considering the poor conditions. *Britannia*, thanks to the extensive Jubilee Tour of the Pacific Islands, New Zealand and Australia, had already steamed 30,000 miles this year and completed her sixth circumnavigation of the world.

The Royal Yacht is an independent command, administered personally by the Flag Officer, Royal Yachts, Rear-Admiral H. P. Janion, an Extra Equerry to the Queen and a member of the Royal Household. *Britannia*'s crew numbers 21 Officers and 250 Yachtsmen, including a Royal Marine Band when royalty is embarked. Officers are normally appointed for two-year periods of duty and half the ratings are permanent crew members who remain for the whole of their service careers; others are attached to the

Yacht for a normal Naval draft. All are volunteers from the Royal Navy, but receive no special benefits in terms of pay, allowances or leave.

Traditions of dress aboard the Royal Yacht include the wearing by the seamen of Naval uniform, with the jumper inside the top of the trousers with a black silk bow at the back. White badges instead of the customary red are worn on blue uniforms, and gym shoes are used extensively.

HMY *Britannia* cost £2·5 million and was built on Clydebank in 1953. She is 413 feet long, of about 5000 tons displacement, and was designed to be a hospital ship in times of war. In peacetime, however, her main function has involved steaming 570,000 miles. In the twenty-four years since commissioning, there have been 24 Commonwealth cruises involving 311 separate ports; 17 state and 60 other foreign visits; and 154 visits to the United Kingdom ports. Not surprising, therefore, that *Britannia* spends more time away from home than the average frigate; in a busy year, as much as 70 per cent of her time is away from Portsmouth, her home port.

As well as enhancing the impact of tours such as those to the United States Bicentennial and the Montreal Olympics last year, *Britannia* takes part in naval exercises, undertakes routine hydrographic tasks at sea and is a regular visitor to Cowes Week. With her blue hull, red waterline, white upper works and buff-coloured masts and funnel, she is probably one of the cleanest and smartest ships afloat.

The final event of the Spithead Review took place in *Ark Royal*, when the Queen was entertained for dinner as a guest of the Commander-in-Chief, Fleet, Admiral Sir Henry Leach. His father, Jack Leach, captained the battleship *Prince of Wales* against the *Bismarck* and was later killed when she was sunk by Japanese bombers. Each of the captains attending the dinner had paid £15 out of his pocket for the privilege. In return, he was allowed to keep his own dinner plate.

The Spithead spectacular: *above*, the Royal party and guests aboard the Royal Yacht *Britannia* on the eve of the Spithead review. *Below*, the review of the fleet is under way and members of the Royal party take the opportunity to photograph and have a closer look at the ships

The fleet ready for inspection: the Queen saw just over a hundred ships of the Royal Navy at the Jubilee Review, almost half the total she saw in 1953 at the Coronation review. (p. 130) *Bottom left*, one of the Valiant-class, nuclear-powered submarines with its complement on parade; *bottom right*, *Sir Winston Churchill*, flagship of the Sail Training Association; (p. 131) *bottom left*, *Britannia* sails through lines of all ships great and small; *bottom right*, the destroyer *Fife*, one of the County-class, guided-missile destroyers

Pictures of the fleet: Princess Anne was one of the more enthusiastic members of the Royal family in capturing the occasion on photographic film. *Top left*, ratings of a County-class destroyer prepare to cheer the Queen; *top right*, members of the crew of the nuclear-powered USS *California*; *centre*, HMS *Hermes*, the anti-submarine and Commando carrier; *bottom*, one of the Royal Navy's new technology vessels, the hovercraft

Her Majesty's ships: after a day spent reviewing her fleet, the Queen was invited aboard the aircraft carrier *Ark Royal* for dinner. Both the Queen and Prince Philip showed great interest in all the ships present for the review

CHAPTER THIRTEEN

Prince Charles in Africa and Canada

Prince Charles also had a busy Jubilee year. In March he went on a two-week African tour, mainly to Ghana where he was the first visiting member of the Royal family since the Queen made a State Visit there in 1961. He toured schools and irrigation schemes, talked to politicians and had a game of polo in Accra. (His team lost 3-2, but he scored both goals.) He put on the striped cotton robe of a tribal chief and was given some presents for the Queen: a hide handbag, a wicker basket and four, red, leather cushions decorated with elephants. In return, he gave them a framed photograph – of himself.

He also went to the Ivory Coast, not an ex-British colony this time but ex-French. President Félix Houphouet-Boigny had invited him when the Ghana visit became known, determined to give him a bigger welcome than his English-speaking neighbours. The Prince replied in French to a speech of welcome by the President, asking his hosts to be indulgent if he massacred the French language. "I hope I may have the opportunity to find, perhaps, a brilliant Ivorian female teacher . . ."

One of the recurring newspaper stories of the year was to marry off Prince Charles. The *Daily Express* had him definitely engaged at least once. Others managed to plan his children's future. Prince Charles himself was amused by the speculation, and made jokes about it in public and private, but he was careful to avoid too many photographs of himself and welcoming dancing girls, just in case the caption writers got really carried away.

In July, Prince Charles went to Canada where he met up with his younger brother Prince Andrew, who was at Lakefield College, one hundred miles north of Toronto at the time. Between them, they provided some of the most amusing Royal pictures of the year, especially when

Prince Charles arrives in Africa for a two-week tour, mainly in Ghana

137

Charles joined in the jollifications at an Indian tribal celebration, smoking peace-pipes and agreeing to have his face painted in red and yellow stripes. He put on a head-dress and played the part very well, but he demurred when a young nubile Indian princess was brought forward to have a war-dance with him.

While in Ghana Prince Charles met many local dignitaries and officials. He was the first member of the Royal family to visit the country since 1961 and he proved to be very popular. At a presentation ceremony Prince Charles found time to don the striped cotton robe of a tribal chief. After Ghana, Charles travelled on to the Ivory Coast where he received an equally warm welcome. He even found one lady wearing a T-shirt carrying a picture of His Royal Highness. He seemed amused to find his bust on her bust

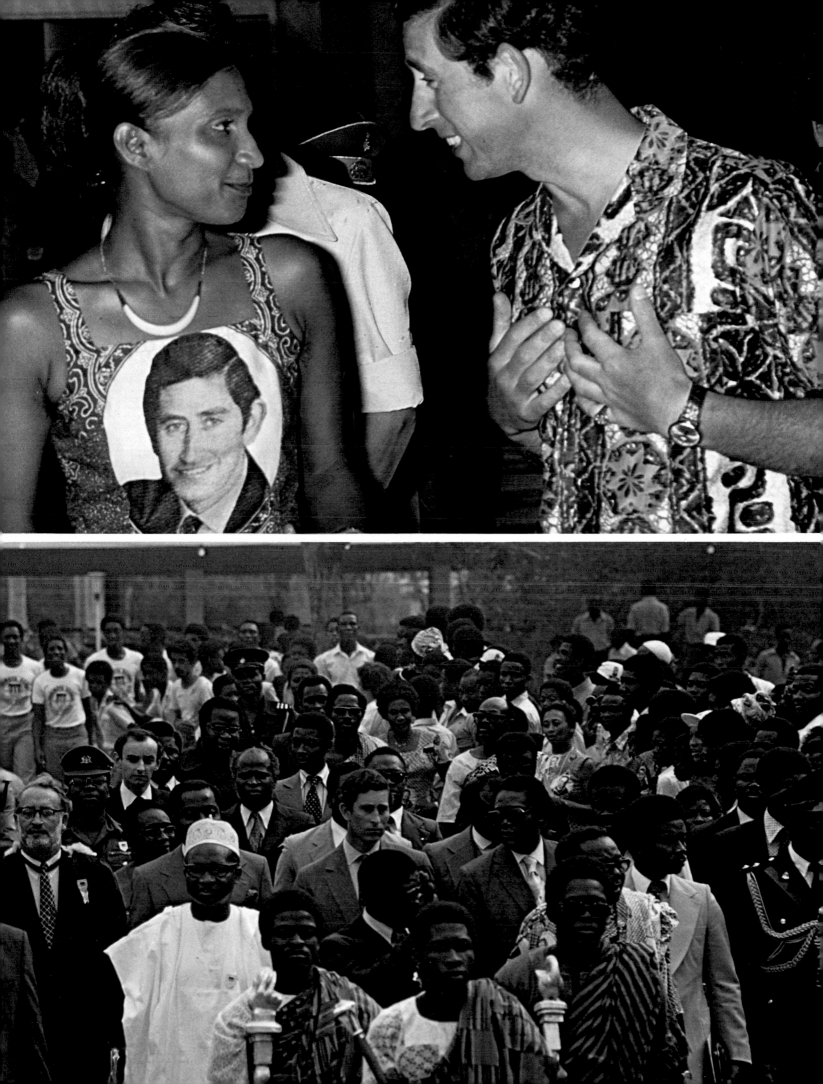

North American jollity: later in the year Prince Charles travelled to Canada where he met up with his younger brother Prince Andrew. It was during this tour that the Royal duo provided some of the most amusing pictures of the year, especially those of Prince Charles fully decorated as a North American Indian. Later, the Royal princes drew the admiration of crowds at a rodeo meeting when they appeared in traditional stetsons and suits

CHAPTER FOURTEEN

Sporting and other highlights

The Queen didn't manage to see Liverpool's famous victory in the European Cup Final, but then she's not known as a football fan. She's not a tennis fan either but she was present when Virginia Wade won the ladies' singles title at Wimbledon. It was the Queen's first visit to Wimbledon since 1962, the year in which Miss Wade made her first, unsuccessful steps. After fifteen years of striving for the title, the nation loved the fact that when she eventually won it the Queen should be there to award the prize. Miss Wade beat Betty Stove of Holland 4-6, 6-3, 6-1, in what was an exciting though not exceptionally good final. She was thought to have played better when she beat the American reigning Wimbledon champion, Chris Evert, in the semi-finals.

The Queen, who prefers horses, managed to see Lester Piggott win the Derby on The Minstrel and also went to Ascot and the Badminton horse trials, but she missed James Hunt winning the British Grand Prix in July. It turned out to be a very successful year for British sport and compared well with the sporting triumphs of her Coronation year, 1953, when Gordon Richards won the Derby and Stanley Matthews turned the Wembley Cup Final into his very own exhibition match. What Coronation year had most of all was the ascent of Everest, a piece of magnificent stage-managing which even the Jubilee organisers couldn't manage, though Princess Anne did choose Jubilee year to announce that she was going to make the Queen a grandmother for the first time.

On the cultural side, the Queen attended a Jubilee Gala performance at Covent Garden in May, and was musically entertained almost everywhere she went on her Jubilee tours, but she attended very few literary or artistic gatherings. She received countless gifts, including a £100,000 Rolls-Royce from a consortium of British companies, a horse from Australia and lots of chairs, cushions and assorted ornaments.

By the look of the photographs, and from first-hand accounts, she perhaps enjoyed her tour of the smaller Pacific islands best of all. It was the beginning of the year and the most informal of the many tours. But everywhere, in Britain and the Commonwealth, her walkabouts were a huge success, even when crowds did break through and endanger her life (as in Scotland) or when she was hit with a placard (as in Australia).

She was seen on Jubilee Day by 500 million TV viewers round the world. In the flesh, counting all her Jubilee touring, at home and abroad, she must have been seen by up to 50 million. Admittedly, if you were stuck at the back of a 100,000 crowd, as outside Buckingham Palace, you didn't see very much, but by doing her walkabouts so assiduously the millions who crowded every route were able to get at least one, brief, fairly reasonable glimpse of the Queen.

London will never see such sights for many years, and the Jubilee certainly provided a lot of fun and brought in a lot of money during some hard times. The tourist invasion was phenomenal, a lot of them spurred on not just by the Jubilee celebrations but by the fall in the value of our currency. Britain suddenly seemed cheap for a holiday, compared with many other countries. The most notable new invasion came from the Arabs. Their spending sprees were talked about all year. Over 200,000 came here during the year, adding to the 30,000 Arabs who were already 'permanent' visitors, buying up million-pound houses, clearing entire jewellery counters at Harrods and ordering clothes in hundreds from Marks and Spencer. In central London, it became a common sight to be completely surrounded in shops by foreign visitors buying everything in triplicate.

During the year, almost everyone bought or was given some sort of Jubilee souvenir. From the first day of Jubilee year, the tills rang to the merry sounds of loyal punters paying far too much money for a load of Jubilee junk. Not all of it was rubbish, of course, but almost all of it was very expensive, certainly much more expensive once some Jubilee label or motif was flashed on to it. Ice lollies, normally 8p each, were being sold to unsuspecting tourists for 30p – this time as Jubilee lollies, just because they happened to be red, white and blue. Marcus Lipton, MP for Lambeth Central, formally complained to the police authorities to stamp out "this blatant exploitation of tourists and to run these ruthless profiteers out of town".

It happened with well-known and well-branded goods. Moët et Chandon champagne, normally selling at £5.15, became £5.75 for exactly the same contents, thanks to the addition of a Jubilee label. Woolworths did a good trade in Jubilee mugs at £1.09, despite competition from their

Jubilee triumph: at long last after fifteen attempts Virginia Wade won the Wimbledon Ladies' Singles Final. In some ways it was the icing to the Jubilee cake. Wimbledon went wild and forgot some of its usual decorum. Tennis fans everywhere managed a sigh of relief. The Queen also attended Badminton for the horse trials

normal mugs, equally decorated but lacking any Jubilee motif, which were on sale at 45p. Tea, which early in the year was 66p a pound, became £2.25 in a Jubilee tin.

More than £4m worth of Jubilee books were on sale or in production at the beginning of the year, consisting of twenty-five different titles, all of them full of old or pre-Jubilee photographs. There was an even larger number of special magazines and booklets. Altogether, it was estimated that £25m worth of Jubilee souvenirs was sold during the year.

Many of the better designed goods were given the seal of approval by the Design Centre in London. A panel, headed by Prince Charles, chose 63 out of 250 souvenirs as being suitably tasteful. Sir Paul Riley, head of the Design Council, said that "Some of the manufacturers couldn't even get the likeness of the Queen right."

The Lord Chamberlain's Office offered general directives to the manufacturers, but had to admit that when it came down to it, they had no control over the use of the Royal arms or royal photographs. The people behind the Muppets (very big in 1977) are able to control the use of their names and images on any objects. Every successful pop group which turns its faces into merchandising will sue for millions if anyone produces a T-shirt or badge without permission. Alas, the Royal family are up for grabs. All that the Lord Chamberlain insisted on was that the production of Jubilee goods should cease on October 1.

North Sea oil kept flowing and our balance of payments began to look a bit healthier, though no one went so far as to say the corner had been turned. Various economic reports and surveys during the year revealed not only that we weren't working hard enough or not producing enough,

After the Jubilee show: members of the Royal Family gather on the balcony of Buckingham Palace to appear before one of the biggest crowds seen in London since the end of the war. From the left, Prince Charles, Prince Edward, Prince Andrew, Lord Mountbatten, Her Majesty the Queen, Prince Philip, Captain Mark Phillips and Princess Anne

but that we actually seemed to be *enjoying* not working hard enough. Ruthless ambition, determination to succeed, striving to get to the top, went out of fashion. Liking one's job, if one could get one, was what mattered, closely followed, perhaps even exceeded, by ample leisure time. Foreign economists tut-tutted, shook their heads and said it wasn't good enough, but in some ways it was the mark of an advanced civilisation. Britain gave the industrial revolution to the world and has moved on to other, perhaps nobler priorities, while the rest of the world was still obsessed by having to produce something. It was noticed during the year that much of Britain's wealth, such as it was, was now coming from invisible earnings, like banking and insurance, and of course tourism.

Tourists certainly got a great deal of pleasure out of the year, as did the 1000 million members of the British Commonwealth of nations who joined together to celebrate the Queen's first twenty-five years. Her Majesty certainly worked hard, visiting twelve different countries (including one foreign country, West Germany, to inspect British troops) and travelling hundreds of thousands of miles. She walked out and met her subjects and they rejoiced in her presence.

The Jubilee didn't help to cure the nation's ills, but it gave people a lot of pleasure. The excuse for the celebrations and street parties and universal coming-together was not that we had survived some terrible war – but that we had survived. Most of all, the Queen had survived twenty-five years as our figurehead. It had all started slowly. There was a feeling that perhaps such frivolities weren't quite right for such serious times. But all the cynics were proved wrong. Jubilee year was the surprise of the decade.

Horses and courses: during the year the Queen found time to follow one of her favourite pastimes, horses. She was at Epsom for the Derby meeting, *top*, and drove in an open landau at Royal Ascot. She was also present at the Windsor horse trials to cheer her son-in-law Captain Mark Phillips who was one of the contestants

Queen's Diary 1977

Christmas 1976 The Queen spends a traditional family Christmas at Windsor.

30 December 1976 Sandringham.

1 February 1977 Returns to Buckingham Palace.

3 February Dinner with Australian High Commissioner at Stoke Lodge, Hyde Park Gate.

8 February The Queen plants an oak tree in the Victoria Embankment gardens. Dinner with New Zealand High Commissioner at New Zealand House.

9 February Departs from Heathrow Airport for visit to Samoa.

14 February Visits Tonga.

16 February Visits Fiji.

22 February Visits New Zealand.

7 March Visits Australia.

23 March Visits Papua–New Guinea.

26 March Returns to Australia.

31 March Returns to London.

7 April Maundy Service at Westminster Abbey.

20 April Presentation of New Colours to 1st Battalion Scots Guards, at Buckingham Palace. Then tree-planting in Hyde Park.

3 May Launching of HMS *Invincible* at Barrow-in-Furness.

6 May Visits the Police at the Peel Centre, Hendon.

7 May Rolls-Royce Parade, Windsor.

10 May Dinner at Buckingham Palace for NATO Foreign Ministers.

15 May Queen is presented with the horse Centennial by the Commissioner of the Royal Canadian Mounted Police at East Lawn, Windsor Castle.

16 May Queen attends the Royal Horticultural Society's Chelsea Show.

17 May Queen and Duke of Edinburgh visit Glasgow, Strathclyde.

18 May Queen and Duke of Edinburgh visit Cumbernauld, Strathclyde and Stirling.

19 May Queen and Duke of Edinburgh visit Perth and Dundee, Tayside.

20 May Queen and Duke of Edinburgh visit Aberdeen, Grampian.

22 May Queen and Duke of Edinburgh arrive at Holyrood House, Edinburgh..

23 May Queen and Duke of Edinburgh visit Edinburgh – reception at Holyrood House for British Commonwealth Ex-Service League Delegates and banquet at Edinburgh Castle.

24 May Opening of Church of Scotland General Assembly, Edinburgh. Visit to sheltered workshop for the blind at Craigmillar. Beating the Retreat at Holyrood House Park followed by banquet.

25 May Church of Scotland General Assembly, Edinburgh; civic lunch followed by Pageant of Scottish Youth in Meadowbank Stadium and performance in King's Theatre.

26 May General Assembly and Free Church of Scotland General Assembly. Followed by garden party at Holyrood House. In evening, serenade in the forecourt of Holyrood House.

27 May Scottish Privileged Bodies present Addresses. Open new terminal building at Edinburgh Airport.

28 May The Queen and the Duke of Edinburgh attend a Gala Performance at the Royal Opera House, Covent Garden.

1 June Queen attends the Epsom Derby.

6 June Queen, accompanied by Duke of Edinburgh, lights the first of a chain of bonfires at Snow Hill, Windsor Great Park.

7 June Queen and Duke of Edinburgh attend a service of thanksgiving for Her Majesty's Silver Jubilee in St Paul's Cathedral. They then attend the Lord Mayor's Banquet luncheon at Guildhall. The Queen makes a broadcast to the Commonwealth.

8 June Commonwealth Heads of Government Conference opens. Banquet and reception for Commonwealth Heads of Government at Buckingham Palace.

9 June Queen and Duke of Edinburgh embark in *Nore* at Greenwich and progress to Lambeth. Review of Fire Brigade, and tea at Lambeth Palace. River pageant and fireworks display.

10 June Reception at Buckingham Palace for Commonwealth officials.

11 June Queen takes the salute at the Queen's Birthday Parade. RAF fly past.

12 June	Queen and Duke of Edinburgh take the salute at a march past of Royal British Legion Standards at Windsor Castle.	13 July	Royal visit to Wakefield, Leeds, Harrogate, York and embark HMY *Britannia* at Hull, Humberside.
13 June	Garter Service at Windsor.	14 July	Royal visit to Cleveland – Middlesbrough, Hartlepool and Stockton. Embark HMY *Britannia* at Tees Dock.
19 June	Queen and Duke of Edinburgh spend the night on board the Royal Train.	15 July	Royal visit to Tyne and Wear. Newcastle, South Shields, Sunderland, Washington and Cramlington.
20 June	Royal visit to Lancaster and Preston, evening entertainment in Manchester. Night on the Royal Train.	18 July	Queen receives Addresses from Privileged Bodies at Windsor.
21 June	Royal visit to Stockport, St Helens. Reception on board HMY *Britannia*. Spend night on Royal Train.	19 July	Garden party at Buckingham Palace. Royal Tournament, Olympia.
22 June	Royal visit to Harlech, Betwys-y-Coed, Llandudno, Bangor and embark HMY *Britannia* at Holyhead to sail to Milford Haven.	21 July	Garden party at Buckingham Palace.
		26 July	Garden party at Buckingham Palace.
23 June	Royal visit to Milford Haven, Haverford West, Carmarthen, Llanelli, Swansea, Margam and re-embark HMY *Britannia* at Barry.	27 July	Royal visit to the West Midlands – Wolverhampton, Dudley, Sandwell, Walsall, Birmingham and Coventry.
24 June	Royal visit to Cardiff, Caerphilly Castle, re-embark HMY *Britannia* at Cardiff. Beating the Retreat.	28 July	Royal visit to Derbyshire – visit to Nottingham. Spend night on the Royal Train.
25 June	Leave HMY *Britannia* for Glamorgan (Rhoose) Airport.	29 July	RAF Review at RAF Finningley, Yorkshire. Fly to Heathrow.
28 June	Naval Review at Spithead, Portsmouth.	2 August	The Queen holds an Investiture.
29 June	Royal visit to Portsmouth. Dinner at Buckingham Palace for Heads of EEC Summit.	4 August	Sail from Southampton in the Royal Yacht.
30 June	Royal drive through South London (Westminster, Kensington and Chelsea, Wandsworth and Lambeth). Tri-Service Musical Pageant at Wembley.	5 August	Disembark from HMY *Britannia* at Torbay to visit Devon. Royal Marine Forces parade in Plymouth.
1 July	Privileged Bodies present Addresses at Buckingham Palace. Royal visit to Wimbledon to mark the centenary of the lawn tennis championship meeting.	6 August	Royal visit to Cornwall – Falmouth, Truro, Bodmin and St Mawes.
		8 August	Royal visit to Avon – Bristol and Bath.
6 July	Drive through North London (Westminster, Camden, Islington, Hackney and Tower Hamlets).	10 August	Royal visit to Northern Ireland.
7 July	Army Review at Sennelager in Federal Republic of Germany.	28 August	Queen and Duke of Edinburgh plant two trees at Crathie Parish Church.
8 July	Privileged Bodies present Addresses at Buckingham Palace.	14 October	Royal visit to Canada – Ottawa.
		19 October	Royal visit to the Bahamas.
11 July	Royal visit to Norfolk, leave from London Airport for Norwich. Embark HMY *Britannia* at Felixstowe.	26 October	Royal visit to the Virgin Islands.
		28 October	Royal visit to Antigua.
12 July	Royal visit to Yorkshire and Humberside – disembark Royal Yacht at Grimsby. Humberside visits to Doncaster, Maltby, Sheffield and Barnsley. Spend night in Royal Train.	31 October	Royal visit to Barbados.
		2 November	Queen and Duke of Edinburgh return to London.
		3 November	State Opening of Parliament.

Meeting the people: the Queen at the Royal Gala, Covent Garden Opera House, and, *top*, with the Royal Canadian Mounted Police at Windsor when she took charge of Centennial, the horse that the Mounties gave Her Majesty back in 1973. Also during the year the Queen inspected the British Army of the Rhine from an open Range Rover

Overleaf: A view from the roof of Buckingham Palace on Jubilee Day with a crowd of over 100,000 chanting ''we want the Queen''

Happy hats: from tiara to headscarf, some of the many hats and smiles which the Queen wore during Jubilee Year 1977

Acknowledgements

Front cover Roger Perry

Page

2 Bruno Barbey
6 John Scott, OPFA
8 Topix
9 Ken Lewis
10 Press Association
14/15 John Scott, OPFA
17 Anwar Hussein
18/19 Anwar Hussein
20/21 Anwar Hussein
22 *Top*, John Scott, OPFA
22 *Bottom*, Anwar Hussein
23 Anwar Hussein
24/25 Anwar Hussein
26/27 John Scott, OPFA
28/29 The Daily Record, Syndication International
30 *Top*, John Scott, OPFA
30 *Bottom*, Anwar Hussein
31 John Scott, OPFA
32 The Daily Record, Syndication International
34/35 Rene Burri
36 Marc Riboud
37 Bryn Campbell
38 *Top*, Rene Burri
38 *Bottom*, Bruno Barbey
39 Robert Freson
40 *Top left*, Robert Freson
40 *Top right*, Bryn Campbell
40 *Centre*, Martine Franck
40 *Bottom*, Henri Cartier-Bresson
41 Bryn Campbell
42/43 Alain le Garsmeur
44 Martine Franck
46/47 Bruno Barbey
48 *Top*, Alain le Garsmeur
48 *Bottom*, Eve Arnold
49 *Top*, Robert Freson
49 *Centre*, Alain le Garsmeur
49 *Bottom*, Alain le Garsmeur
50 *Top*, Alain le Garsmeur
50 *Bottom*, Eve Arnold
51 *Top*, Alain le Garsmeur
51 *Bottom*, Donald McCullin
52/53 Alain le Garsmeur
54/55 Bryn Campbell
56 Robert Freson
57 *Top*, Bryn Campbell
57 *Bottom*, Marc Riboud
58 Robert Freson
60 Rene Burri
61 Ian Yeomans
62 *Top left*, Ian Yeomans
62 *Bottom left*, Ian Yeomans
62/63 Fox Photos

64/65 Ian Yeomans
66 *Top left*, Robert Freson
66 *Top right*, Marc Riboud
66 *Bottom left*, Robert Freson
66 *Bottom right*, Robert Freson
67 Donald McCullin
68 *Top*, Roger Perry
68 *Bottom*, Bryn Campbell
69 *Top*, Donald McCullin
69 *Centre*, Roger Perry
69 *Bottom*, Donald McCullin
70 *Top*, Donald McCullin
70 *Bottom*, Roger Perry
72/73 David Reed
74 *Top*, Alain le Garsmeur
74 *Bottom*, Bryn Campbell
75 *Top*, Bryn Campbell
75 *Bottom*, Bruno Barbey
76/77 Kenneth Griffiths
78 Kenneth Griffiths
79 *Top left*, Robert Freson
79 *Top right*, Robert Freson
79 *Bottom*, Kenneth Griffiths
80/81 Kenneth Griffiths
82/83 Robert Freson
84/85 *Left*, Bruno Barbey
85 *Top right*, Eve Arnold
85 *Bottom right*, Eve Arnold
86 *Top left*, Bryn Campbell
86 *Centre left*, Marc Riboud
86 *Bottom left*, Ian Berry
86 *Top right*, Robert Freson
87 *Top left*, Robert Freson
87 *Top centre*, Eve Arnold
87 *Top right*, Robert Freson
87 *Bottom*, Kenneth Griffiths
88/89 Ian Berry
89 *Top right*, Ian Berry
89 *Bottom left*, Robert Freson
90 *Top left*, Mary Hodges
90 *Centre left*, Ian Berry
90 *Bottom left*, Roger Perry
90 *Top right*, Colin Jones
92/93 Press Association
94/94 Press Association
96 Central Press
97 Anwar Hussein
98/99 Bryn Campbell
100/101 Bryn Campbell
102 *Top*, Bruno Barbey
102 *Bottom*, Donald McCullin
103 Bryn Campbell
104/105 Rene Burri
106 *Top*, Bryn Campbell
106 *Bottom*, Robert Freson
107 Bryn Campbell
108 *Top*, Bruno Barbey

108 *Bottom*, Bryn Campbell
110 *Top*, Robert Freson
110 *Bottom*, Roger Perry
111 Robert Freson
112 Anwar Hussein
114/115 Anwar Hussein
116/117 Central Press
117 *Right*, Syndication International
118/119 Fox Photos
120/121 Press Association
122/123 Press Association
124/125 Press Association
126 *Top*, Press Association
126 *Centre*, Press Association
126 *Bottom*, Les Wilson
127 Press Association
129 *Top*, Bryn Campbell
129 *Bottom*, Fox Photos
130/131 Georg Gerster
130 *Bottom left*, Bryn Campbell
130 *Bottom right*, Bryn Campbell
131 *Bottom left*, Bryn Campbell
131 *Bottom right*, Bryn Campbell
132 Fox Photos
133 Bryn Campbell
134 *Top*, Roger Perry
134 *Bottom*, Daily Mail
135 Daily Mail
136/137 Anwar Hussein
138/139 Anwar Hussein
140/141 Anwar Hussein
142/143 Anwar Hussein
144 Anwar Hussein
146 Sport and General
147 Anwar Hussein
148/149 Fox Photos
150 *Top*, Fox Photos
150 *Bottom*, Central Press
151 *Top*, Anwar Hussein
151 *Bottom*, John Scott, OPFA
154 Fox Photos
155 *Top*, John Scott, OPFA
155 *Bottom*, Press Association
156/157 Keystone PA
158/159 Anwar Hussein
Back cover Ian Berry

Editor and Author: Hunter Davies

Picture Editors: Vincent Page and June Stanier

Production Editor: John Houston

Research: Rosemary Atkins and Christine Walker